TREKKING IN AUSTRIA'S ZILLERTAL ALPS

THE ZILLERTAL RUCKSACK ROUTE, SOUTH TIROL TOUR, PETER HABELER AND OLPERER RUNDE

by Allan Hartley

JUNIPER HOUSE, MURLEY MOSS,
OXENHOLME ROAD, KENDAL, CUMBRIA LA9 7RL
www.cicerone.co.uk

© Allan Hartley 2023
Third edition 2023
ISBN: 978 1 78631 063 7
Second edition 2013
First edition 2003

Printed in Turkey by Pelikan Basim using responsibly sourced paper.
A catalogue record for this book is available from the British Library.

Route mapping by Lovell Johns www.lovelljohns.com
All photographs are by the author unless otherwise stated.
Contains OpenStreetMap.org data © OpenStreetMap
contributors, CC-BY-SA. NASA relief data courtesy of ESRI

Acknowledgements

To the many members of the Austrian Alpine Club (UK) who have accompanied
me on trips to the Zillertal over several decades.

*This book is dedicated to my late wife Marilyn and our mutual friend Helmut
Meier, a dear friend and companion on many an alpine journey, who was sadly
killed in a tragic accident while descending from the Dristner in the Zillertal.*

Note on mapping

The route maps in this guide are derived from publicly available data, data-
bases and crowd-sourced data. As such they have not been through the
detailed checking procedures that would generally be applied to a published
map from an official mapping agency. However, we have reviewed them
closely in the light of local knowledge as part of the preparation of this guide.

Front cover: At Furtschaglhaus looking towards the Grosser Moeseler 3480m
(ZRR Stage 5)

CONTENTS

Map key 6
Route summary tables 8

INTRODUCTION 13
The Zillertal valley 16
Mayrhofen 16
When to go 18
Getting there and back 20
Places to stay 24
Local transport 26
Local services 26
Peter Habeler's Office (mountain guides) 27
Children 27
The Austrian Alpine Club OeAV 28
Huts 30
Hut meals and menus 34
Kit list 35
Route finding 38
Maps 39
Alpine walking skills 40
Glaciers and glacier travel 40
Health and safety 42
Electronic devices 44
Using this guide 45

ZILLERTAL RUCKSACK ROUTE 49
Trek 1   Zillertal Rucksack Route 50
Stage 1   Mayrhofen to Karl von Edel Hut 54
Excursion: Ascent of Ahornspitze (2973m) 57
Stage 2   Karl von Edel Hut to Kasseler Hut 59
Excursion: Ascent of Wollbachspitze (3210m) south-west ridge 65
Excursion: Ascent of Gruene Wand Spitze (2946m) 67
Stage 3   Kasseler Hut to Greizer Hut 69
Excursion: Ascent of Grosser Loeffler (3379m) 73
Stage 4   Greizer Hut to Berliner Hut 76
Stage 4A Greizer Hut to Berliner Hut via Floitenkees glacier
            or Schwarzenstein Hut 84
Excursion: Ascent of the Berliner Spitze (Hornspitze III) (3254m) 87

Stage 5   Berliner Hut to Furtschaglhaus 90
Excursion: Ascent of Grosser Moeseler (3480m) via the west spur 95
Stage 6   Furtschaglhaus to Olperer Hut 98
Stage 6A Furtschaglhaus to Olperer Hut via Pfitscherjochhaus 104
Excursion: Ascent of Olperer (3476m) via Schneegupf south-east ridge 106
Stage 7   Olperer Hut to Friesenberghaus 110
Excursion: Ascent of Hoher Riffler (3168m) 113
Excursion: Ascent of Peterskoepfl (2679m) 116
Stage 8   Friesenberghaus to Gams Hut 118
Excursion: Ascent of Vordere Grinbergspitze (2765m) 123
Stage 9   Gams Hut to Ginzling and Mayrhofen 126
Stage 9A Gams Hut to Finkenberg and Mayrhofen 129

PETER HABELER AND OLPERER RUNDE TOURS 130
Trek 2   Peter Habeler Runde 132
Stage 1   Touristenrast Gasthof to Landshuter Europa Hut 134
Stage 2   Landshuter Europa Hut to Pfitscherjochhaus 139
Stage 3   Pfitscherjochhaus to Olperer Hut 142
Stage 4   Olperer Hut to Friesenberghaus 145
Stage 5   Friesenberghaus to Tuxerjochhaus via Friesenbergscharte 146
Stage 6   Tuxerjochhaus to Geraer Hut 151
Stage 7   Geraer Hut to Touristenrast Gasthof 154
Trek 3   Olperer Runde Tour 156

ZILLERTAL SOUTH TIROL TOUR 159
Trek 4   Zillertal South Tirol Tour 160
Stage 1   Touristenrast Gasthof to Geraer Hut 165
Stage 2   Geraer Hut to Pfitscherjochhaus 166
Stage 3   Pfitscherjochhaus to Hochfeiler Hut 171
Excursion: Ascent of Hochfeiler (3510m) 174
Stage 4   Hochfeiler Hut to Edelraut Hut 176
Stage 5   Edelraut Hut to Nevesjoch Hut 181
Excursion: Ascent of Grosser Moeseler (3480m) 184
Stage 6   Nevesjoch Hut to Schwarzenstein Hut 186
Stage 7   Schwarzenstein Hut to Berliner Hut or Greizer Hut 193

HUT DIRECTORY 197
Berliner Hut (2042m) 199
Dominikus Hut Alpengasthof (1805m) 203
Edelraut Hut (2545m) 204

Friesenberghaus (2498m) 207
Furtschaglhaus (2295m) 210
Gams Hut (1916m). 212
Gasthof Stein (1555m) 215
Geraer Hut (2326m). 216
Greizer Hut (2226m) 219
Hochfeiler Hut (2710m) 221
Kasseler Hut (2177m) 224
Karl von Edel Hut (2238m) 226
Landshuter Europa Hut (2693m) 228
Nevesjoch Hut (2420m) 231
Olperer Hut (2389m) 233
Pfitscherjochhaus (2275m) 236
Schwarzenstein Hut (3027m) 239
Tuxerjochhaus (2316m) 241

Appendix A   Useful contacts. 244
Appendix B   German–English glossary 248
Appendix C   Further reading. 251

Updates to this guide

While every effort is made by our authors to ensure the accuracy of guidebooks as they go to print, changes can occur during the lifetime of an edition. This guidebook was researched and written during the COVID-19 pandemic. While we are not aware of any significant changes to routes or facilities at the time of printing, it is likely that the current situation will give rise to more changes than would usually be expected. Any updates that we know of for this guide will be on the Cicerone website (www.cicerone. co.uk/1063/updates), so please check before planning your trip. We also advise that you check information about such things as transport, accommodation and shops locally. Even rights of way can be altered over time.

We are always grateful for information about any discrepancies between a guidebook and the facts on the ground, sent by email to updates@cicerone.co.uk or by post to Cicerone, Juniper House, Murley Moss, Oxenholme Road, Kendal, LA9 7RL.

Register your book: To sign up to receive free updates, special offers and GPX files where available, register your book at www.cicerone.co.uk.

Symbols used on route maps

~	route
- - -	alternative route
~	excursion
(S)	start point
(F)	finish point
(SF)	start/finish point
(F)	alternative finish point
➤	route direction
	glacier
	crevasse field
	woodland
	urban areas
	international border
—■—	station/railway
■	bus stop
⬒	cable car
P	parking
▲	peak
⬆	manned hut
⬆	other accommodation
■	building
♦ ✝	church/cathedral
⤨	pass
=	footbridge
•	water feature
✳	viewpoint
❶	technical/hazardous section (fixed ropes, wires, ladders, crevasses)
·	other feature
⚑SP	signpost

Relief
in metres

4000 and above
3800–4000
3600–3800
3400–3600
3200–3400
3000–3200
2800–3000
2600–2800
2400–2600
2200–2400
2000–2200
1800–2000
1600–1800
1400–1600
1200–1400
1000–1200
800–1000
600–800
400–600
200–400
0–200

SCALE: 1:50,000

0 kilometres 0.5   1
0 miles   0.5

Contour lines are drawn at 25m intervals and highlighted at 100m intervals.

GPX files for all routes can be downloaded free at www.cicerone.co.uk/1063/GPX.

Mountain safety

Every mountain walk has its dangers, and those described in this guidebook are no exception. All who walk or climb in the mountains should recognise this and take responsibility for themselves and their companions along the way. The author and publisher have made every effort to ensure that the information contained in this guide was correct when it went to press, but, except for any liability that cannot be excluded by law, they cannot accept responsibility for any loss, injury or inconvenience sustained by any person using this book.

International distress signal *(emergency only)*
Six blasts on a whistle (and flashes with a torch after dark) spaced evenly for one minute, followed by a minute's pause. Repeat until an answer is received. The response is three signals per minute followed by a minute's pause.

Helicopter rescue
The following signals are used to communicate with a helicopter:

Help needed:
raise both arms
above head to
form a 'Y'

Help not needed:
raise one arm
above head, extend
other arm downward to
form the diagonal of an N

Should you be involved with a helicopter rescue...
* Stay at least 50m+ from the helicopter.
* Do not approach the helicopter unless signalled by the winch man to do so.
* Do not approach the helicopter from behind.
* Ensure that all loose items of quipment are made secure.

Emergency telephone numbers
The following numbers can be dialled from a mobile phone even when the phone indicated that there is no reception from your service provider. Fortunately, in Austria mobile phone reception is excellent.
* Mountain Rescue (Bergrettung) Austria 140
* Mountain Rescue (Buergrettung) Italy 118
* Red Cross (Rotes Kreutz) 144
* European emergency telephone number 112

ROUTE SUMMARY TABLES

Stage	Start	Distance	Ascent	Descent	Time	Page
Zillertal Rucksack Route						
Stage 1	Mayrhofen	4km	285m	negligible	3hr	54
Stage 2	Karl von Edel Hut	12.5km	750m	800m	8–10hr	59
Stage 3	Kasseler Hut	9.25km	750m	690m	6–7hr	69
Stage 4	Greizer Hut	9km	1050m	1230m	6–8hr	76
Stage 4A	Greizer Hut	12.75km	1100m	1150m	8–10hr	84
Stage 5	Berliner Hut	8km	1020m	850m	6–7hr	90
Stage 6	Furtschaglhaus	9.25km	600m	500m	5–6hr	98
Stage 6A	Furtschaglhaus	13km + 8.5km	480m + 580m	300m + 400m	2 days (4–5hr + 6hr)	104
Stage 7	Olperer Hut	4km	290m	200m	2½–3hr	110
Stage 8	Friesenberghaus	13.5km	600m	1100m	10–12hr	118
Stage 9	Gams Hut	7km	negligible	950m	3hr	126
Stage 9A	Gams Hut	10km	negligible	1030m	2hr	129
Total		**79.5km**	**6445m**	**8500m**	**9 days**	

Zillertal Rucksack Route optional excursions

Ascent	Start	Distance	Ascent/descent	Time	Grade	Page
Ahornspitze	Karl von Edel Hut	3km	735m	ascent 2–2½hr, descent 1–1½hr	F	57
Wollbachspitze	Kasseler Hut	8km	1030m	ascent 4hr, descent 3hr	F+	65
Gruene Wand Spitze	Kasseler Hut	6km	770m	ascent 3hr, descent 2¼hr	F+	67
Grosser Loeffler	Greizer Hut	8km	1155m	ascent 5hr, descent 4hr	PD+	73
Berliner Spitze	Berliner Hut	8km	1215m	ascent 4–5hr, descent 3–4hr	PD–	87
Grosser Moeseler	Furtschaglhaus	6km	1185m	ascent 4–5hr, descent 3–4hr	PD	95
Olperer	Olperer Hut	6km	1100m	ascent 4–5hr, descent 3hr	PD	106
Hoher Riffler	Friesenberghaus	4km	750m	ascent 3½hr, descent 2½hr	F–	113
Peterskoepfl	Friesenberghaus	2km	200m	ascent ¾hr, descent ½hr	F–	116
Vordere Grinbergspitze	Gams Hut	4km	825m	ascent 3hr, descent 1½hr	F	123

Peter Habeler Runde

Stage	Start	Distance	Ascent	Descent	Time	Page
Stage 1	Touristenrast Gasthof	8km	1300m	100m	5–6hr	134
Stage 2	Landshuter Europa Hut	7.5km	250m	650m	3–4hr	139
Stage 3	Pfitscherjochhaus	8.5km	580m	400m	5hr	142
Stage 4	Olperer Hut	4km	200m	190m	2½–3hr	145
Stage 5	Friesenberghaus	8.75km	620m	650m	6–7hr	146

9

Stage	Start	Distance	Ascent	Descent	Time	Page
Stage 6	Tuxerjochhaus	9.25km	620m	750m	6–7hr	151
Stage 7	Geraer Hut	7.5km	negligible	980m	2½–3hr	154
Total		**53.5km**	**3570m**	**3720m**	**7 days**	

Olperer Runde

Stage	Start	Distance	Ascent	Descent	Time	Page
Stage 1	Touristenrast Gasthof	8km	930m	negligible	3–4hr	157
Stage 2	Geraer Hut	7.5km	750m	700m	7–8hr	157
Stage 3	Olperer Hut	4km	200m	190m	2½–3hr	158
Stage 4	Friesenberghaus	8.75km	620m	650m	6–7hr	158
Stage 5	Tuxerjochhaus	9.25km	620m	750m	6–7hr	158
Stage 6	Geraer Hut	7.5km	negligible	980m	2½–3hr	158
Total		**45km**	**3120m**	**3270m**	**6 days**	

Zillertal South Tirol Tour

Stage	Start	Distance	Ascent	Descent	Time	Page
Stage 1	Touristenrast Gasthof	8km	800m	negligible	3–4hr	165
Stage 2	Geraer Hut	10.25km	1300m	970m	6–7hr	166
Stage 3	Pfitscherjochhaus	9km	900m	530m	6–7hr	171
Stage 4	Hochfeiler Hut	4km	250m	430m	3hr	176

Stage	Start	Distance	Ascent	Descent	Time	Page
Stage 5	Edelraut Hut	9km	200m	100m	3–5hr	181
Stage 6	Nevesjoch Hut	12km	1350m	1060m	8–10hr	186
Stage 7	Schwarzenstein Hut	8.75km/ 5.25km	210m/negligible	880m/700m	6hr/3–4hr	193
Total		**61km**	**5010m**	**4670m**	**7 days**	

Zillertal South Tirol Tour optional excursions

Ascent	Start	Distance	Ascent/descent	Time	Grade	Page
Hochfeiler	Hochfeiler Hut	4km	800m	ascent 3–4hr, descent 2–2½hr	F+	174
Grosser Moeseler	Nevesjoch Hut	11km	1100m	ascent 4–5hr, descent 3hr	PD+	184

Summit views from the Hochfeiler (3510m), an optional extension on the Zillertal South Tirol Tour (ZSTT Stage 3)

INTRODUCTION

Berliner Hut (ZRR Stages 4/4A, ZSTT Stage 7)

Mayrhofen, the pristine holiday resort nestling deep withing the Zillertal valley is justifiably very popular with walkers, climbers and mountain lovers alike for there is something for everyone to do and plenty to explore. With more than a dozen quality mountain huts dotted around the Zillertal, there is plenty of scope for mountain-wandering adventures with the opportunity to spend many a night in spectacular, lofty locations, making the Zillertal Alps a hard-to-resist location.

The Zillertal Alps are located entirely within the Austrian province of the Tirol. To the east, the Zillertal merges with the mountains of the Reichen and Venediger groups and the province of the East Tirol, to the west lies the Brenner pass into Italy and the mountains of the Stubai Alps. Southwards are Italy and the South Tirol, along with the mountains at the head of the Zillertal valley, which, together with its huts, were annexed to Italy at the end of World War 1. To the north is the Inn valley, which runs the entire length of the Tirol, the Zillertal being the longest subsidiary valley in the Tirol at some 50km long, terminating at its head at the picturesque and popular holiday resort town of Mayrhofen.

Above Mayrhofen the main Zillertal valley splits off into a number of subsidiary valleys all ending with the word *grund*, and they in turn branch off in various directions. To the east is the steeply sided Zillergrund valley, flanked by the Ahornspitze and Brandberger Kolm, with the village of Brandberg and the farming hamlets of Inder Au and Baerenbad leading to the Zillergrund reservoir and the old cattle drovers' trail into the Ahrntal valley of Italy and the South Tirol.

To the west the road leads to the villages of Finkenberg and Hintertux and the mountains of the Tuxer Hauptkamm and the Hintertux valley, flanked by the peaks of the Grinbergspitze to the south and Tuxer Alpen to the north with the Penkenjoch and Rastkogel. To the south-west is the main Zamsergrund valley and the delightful village of Ginzling and the hamlet of Breitlahner, beyond which the road terminates at the head of the Zamsergrund valley by the Schlegeisspeicher hydroelectric reservoir and the ancient trade route into the Pfitschertal valley of Italy and the South Tirol via Pfitscherjoch.

Immediately to the south of Mayrhofen, the peaks of the Ahornspitze, Dristner and the bulk of the Grinbergspitze stand tall and are unmistakeable from the railway station. Above the treeline the horizon to the south is dominated by the peaks that span the border of Italy and the South Tirol, particularly the Hochfeiler, Grosser Moeseler and Schwarzenstein, names and features that will become familiar during the course of the mountain excursions detailed in this guide.

THE ZILLERTAL RUCKSACK ROUTE

The Zillertal Rucksack Route, also known as the Berliner Hoehenweg or the Zillertaler Runde, starts from the Karl von Edel Hut above Mayrhofen and visits each of the following huts in turn, the Kasseler, Greizer, Berliner, Furtschaglhaus, Olperer and Friesenberghaus, ending at the Gams Hut high above the charming villages of Ginzling and Finkenberg.

This gives a continuous walk of about ten days, which can be extended to include ascents of the local peaks, *Klettersteig* (via ferrata) rock-scramble adventures or simple rest days.

As the name suggests, the Rucksack Route can be traversed entirely without the need to cross glaciers or have specialist climbing skills. However, you will still have to negotiate steep ground, cross late-summer snow and make use of fixed wire ropes here and there, installed to aid your stability.

Some Alpine flowers that you might see: (clockwise from top) Stemless gentian; round-headed rampion (devil's claw); alpine aster; martagon Lily

The Zillertal's highest peak is the Hochfeiler (3510m), with a further 40 peaks over 3000m, many of which are glaciated or have permanent snow cover.

The Zillertal area provides ample opportunity for all mountain enthusiasts. It is ideal for first-time visitors to the Alps, particularly aspiring alpinists and family groups with children. However, it is important to remember that the Zillertal is not necessarily a tame area in comparison with the Western Alps, as these mountains can challenge even the most experienced.

Whatever your aspirations you will not be disappointed.

Gruss Gott und Sehr Gut Zillerbergtouren.

THE ZILLERTAL VALLEY

From the entrance of the valley at Strass to its head at Mayrhofen, the Zillertal valley with its pretty chalet-style houses is some 50km long of organised Tirolean charm. As you travel further up the valley, you will pass through the charming villages of Schlitters, Fuegen-Hart, Kaltenbach-Stumm, Zell am Ziller, Hippach-Ramsau and lastly Mayrhofen the Zillertal's main village-cum-town and commercial centre with the main peaks of the Zillertal mountains at its head.

MAYRHOFEN

The delightful town of Mayrhofen, one of the premier holiday resorts in the Tirol, is wholly geared up for summer and winter tourism to suit all tastes and budgets. However, it should come as no surprise that development came late to Mayrhofen, it being located some 50km up a dead-end valley in the middle of nowhere, isolated from the main communication links of the Inn valley. While the Romans showed interest and various wandering tribes came and went, the problems of access for trade made it difficult for settlements to establish themselves in the valley.

Named after a few farms at the head of the valley, Mayrhofen started to feature in rural affairs at the start of the eighteenth century, but it didn't feature seriously in anything other than farming and as a good place to hunt and collect minerals. Its isolation was no defence during the Napoleonic wars of 1809, when the Zillertal menfolk picked up their arms and opted to fight against the French and the Bavarians with the Tirolean folklore hero, Andreas Hofer. Sadly, they lost this fight, which resulted in the Bavarians ruling the Tirol for the next few years.

By 1816 Napoleon had been defeated. The Tirol was handed back to its rightful owners, with all the provinces united under the Royal Household of Emperor Franz Joseph I. With the war over, almost another 50 years would pass before tourism and mountain wandering became part of the local economy with the establishment of the Austrian Alpine Club, the

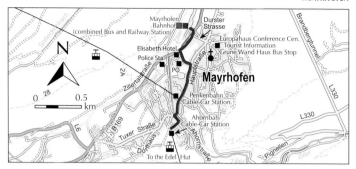

OeAV, in 1862 and the opening of the Berliner Hut in 1879.

Construction of the railway in 1902, which was built to support forestry and the transportation of minerals and magnesite ore from the lucrative mines of Hintertux, opened up the Zillertal valley immensely. Since then, Mayrhofen has grown steadily from the wealth created by the Zillertal valley from agriculture, farming and forestry but, above all, from tourism.

Mayrhofen's weather conundrum

Mayrhofen, and the Zillertal in general, can be a pretty miserable place should you be unfortunate to have indifferent weather, for the clouds just

Street scene in Mayrhofen

swirl around and refuse to budge from our beloved peaks.

If the Ahornsptize has a raised hat, the weather will be good. If the hat is pulled down over his ears, the weather will be bad!

This can be a miserable experience, particularly if you have children with you, so other than the normal theme park activities, what to do? Here are some suggestions:

- **Rattenberg** – This delightful, small medieval town, with quirky timber-framed buildings and cobbled streets, is famous for its handmade glass. Take the train to Jenbach then the local bus service to Brixlegg and Rattenberg.
- **Schwaz medieval silver mine** – Take the train to Jenbach, then the regional train heading to Innsbruck, getting off at Schwaz; thereafter, it is a short walk to the visitor centre. See www. silberbergwerk.at.
- **Ziller river** – White water rafting is great after rain, when the Ziller is in flood. Reservation offices can be found in Mayrhofen.
- **Klettersteig** – The conditions needs to be dry, but those of you armed with climbing tackle may find some consolation in indifferent weather by trying the *Klettersteig*, via ferrata–type protected climbing routes, which start near Gasthof Zillertal, not far from the railway station on the west side of the river.

- **Innsbruck** – Capital city of the province of Tirol, Innsbruck, named after the river on which it stands, is overlooked by the Karwendel range of mountains and is famous as a centre for Winter Olympic sports. The city is well worth a visit in its own right, particularly the *Alte Stadt* (old town), but also the OeAV Alpenverein Museum; located within the Hofburg Imperial Palace in the old town, it has many fine exhibits from alpinism's golden era, perhaps the most notable being memorabilia of Hermann Buehl's ascent of Nanga Parbat in the Karakoram Mountains of northern Pakistan. The museum is open Monday to Saturday during normal business hours. Take the train to Jenbach, followed by the regional train to Innsbruck. It is a 10-minute walk thereafter from the *Hauptbahnhof* (main railway station) to the old town.

WHEN TO GO

The summer season usually starts in mid June and ends in late September.

June is early season and not the best time to visit as it is not unusual to find large amounts of old snow lying on the north-facing slopes, such as on the Lapenscharte.

In July, the weather will be warmer and the winter snow will have receded further, although there will be more people in the mountains and at the huts.

August is seen as the peak season, when most Europeans take their holidays and the huts will be at their busiest. The weather is at its most settled, although it is not unusual to see cloud build up late morning and thunderstorms appear in the evening. As an aside, August is when most of the villages in the Zillertal hold their summer church festivals, known as *Kirchentage*. They are extremely good fun and it is well worth making a visit to villages such as Stumm and Finkenberg, which will be set up

Typical signage by the Alpenverein Suedtirol (AVS) for routes in the South Tirol

with market stalls, street entertainment, local crafts and lots of music for a fun family day out.

September announces the arrival of autumn, and the weather will be cooler and the huts quieter as the end of the season approaches.

The author's personal choice for a two-week holiday is either the middle of July or the first two weeks in September.

GETTING THERE AND BACK

Getting to Austria is relatively straightforward no matter how you travel. In all cases, your first point of contact with the Zillertal valley is at the major road and railway intersection at the industrial town of Jenbach in the Inn valley. Thereafter, the one-hour, 50km (30 mile) journey up the Zillertal valley, by road or rail, leads to the resort town of Mayrhofen, the starting point of your Zillertal experience.

By rail

Consult the Eurostar website (www. eurostar.com/uk-en), but the two most commonly used routes from the UK are as follows. Each route will get you to Innsbruck and Jenbach within 18 hours of leaving London.
- London–Dover–Calais–Paris–Zurich–Innsbruck–Jenbach
- London–Dover–Ostend–Brussels–Munich–Jenbach
  See the internet for further details.

If travelling from outside the UK, take transport links to Innsbruck or

Munich for onward connections to Jenbach. The 'Onward travel' section below details transport links between Jenbach and Mayrhofen.

By road
For the most direct route by road from the UK, take the Dover–Ostend channel crossing, then take the motorways to Munich and into Austria at Kufstein, followed by the short drive up the Inn valley to Jenbach and Mayrhofen. Whatever your chosen route, consult with your motoring organisation, such as the AA or RAC, before setting out. If there is more than one driver, it is just about possible to get to Mayrhofen within 24 hours from Calais or Ostend.

It is important when parking your car to consider how you will get back to it for the return journey; this is not always easy if you are forced to drop down into another valley. It is advisable to leave your car in Jenbach or one of the other major villages that have good bus or railway connections to and from Mayrhofen.

Suggested route from Dover: Lille–Luxembourg–Saarbrucken–Pirmasens–Bad Bergzabern–Karlsruhl–Stuttgard–Munich–Kufstein–Jenbach–Mayrhofen.

See www.adac.de and www.oeamtc.at.

By air
Note that even if you travel by air, which is without doubt the quickest way to get to Austria and the Zillertal, you may not have sufficient time,

leaving the UK early morning, to catch a train to Jenbach and Mayrhofen and reach one of the huts before nightfall. At best, you should plan to stay overnight in Mayrhofen and continue your journey the next day. However, if you are travelling light and have no hold-ups, it is just about possible to get to the Edel Hut by early evening.

Flights
The traditional routes from the UK are as follows: London–Munich, Manchester–Munich, Birmingham–Munich, London–Salzburg and London–Innsbruck. Some of the major operators, particularly Lufthansa, have several flights a day from London, Manchester, Birmingham and Glasgow. Other budget carriers also operate from London City, Luton, Gatwick and Stansted.

The international airports of Munich, Salzburg and Innsbruck are also well served by flights from many other international airports. See Appendix A for airline websites.

Of course, travelling by air gets you to mainland Europe quickly, but you may lose precious time transferring to the *Hauptbahnhof* (railway station), and you may experience frustrating delays and hold-ups just finding your way about.

Onward travel

From Munich
Munich International Airport has a direct connection with the regional

The Zillertal Railway's 'Puffing Billy' steam train; note the Penkenbahn cable car in the background

railway network, and there are frequent trains, every 30 minutes or so. Follow the train signs marked 'DB' and 'S'. This is a similar set-up to the London Underground, which means you need to purchase a ticket before getting on the train. There is also a railway booking office in the airport arrivals hall, adjacent to the hotel reservations and car hire concession counters; here you can buy your ticket to Jenbach, *hin und zuruck* (round trip). Frequent express trains run every two hours or so. Once you are on your journey, you will need to get off the regional train at Muenchen Ost (Munich East); listen to the announcements and change platforms to get on one of the intercity trains, *schnell zug* (fast train). Look out for the matrix signboards at the station and on the side of the trains and board the first one that shows Innsbruck or Brennero or Venezia (Venedig in German) – any destination heading into Italy or Switzerland will do, as they all have to go via Jenbach.

There is also a DB ticket office at Munich East station; you will find the ticket office at road level, alongside shops and fast-food outlets. With express trains it is also possible to pay on the train, sometimes at a premium.

Train tickets can also be purchased in advance and online by visiting www.bahn.de. Click on the dropdown menu to access the website in English.

From Salzburg

At Salzburg Airport take the 'Line 2' bus service to the railway station, from where a train ticket can be purchased to Jenbach. The journey time, travelling west along the Inn valley, is just over one hour.

From Innsbruck

At Innsbruck Airport a bus service, as well as taxis, will get you to Innsbruck city centre and the *Hauptbahnhof* (railway station), where you can access the regional train service to Jenbach.

From Jenbach

At Jenbach there is a local bus service and a narrow-gauge railway to the road head at Mayrhofen; this journey takes about one hour. The last train to Mayrhofen is currently at 20:07 and the last bus is at 21:15. See www.zillertalbahn.at and www.vvt.at for details.

Jenbach is home to the Zillertal railway and its collection of old steam locomotives, known as the *Dampfzug*. But, more famed as 'Thomas the Tank Engine' or simply 'Puffing Billy', these charming little trains are every kid's delight. One of these little trains travels up and down the Zillertal valley throughout the season, pulling behind it 100-year-old, bright-red carriages. If you have children with you, the steam train is a fitting way to start or end your journey in the Zillertal. Just two steam trains operate per day, and many of the seats are reserved in advance so plan your journey well.

- Jenbach–Mayrhofen 10:42
- Mayrhofen–Jenbach 14:43

Airport transfers

A further alternative is to make a reservation with the Four Seasons Travel Company (www.tirol-taxi.at, tel 0043 512 584157), who specialise in coach or minibus transfers to and from Munich and Salzburg airports to Innsbruck. If you are a group of eight, for example, this can be more cost and time effective, as you will be collected at the airport and driven straight to your destination in Mayrhofen. Otherwise, if you are a two or a three, make a reservation on one their luxury coaches.

The return journey

This note is mainly for people travelling by air rather than those travelling by road and rail; you will need to devote the last day of your vacation to making the journey home.

The journey time from Mayrhofen to Munich Airport is around 2½hr, to Salzburg Airport 2hr and to Innsbruck Airport 2hr.

The first train from Mayrhofen to Jenbach is at 06:30; thereafter, the timings are roughly every half hour from 06:50 onwards.

The earliest train from Jenbach to Munich is at 08:07 then 09:02 and 10:57. Remember to change trains at Munich East station and get on the regional shuttle train service S8 marked 'Flughafen'.

From Jenbach the train times to Salzburg are roughly every two hours: 09:26/11:26.

See Appendix A for transport providers and their websites, and Appendix B for a glossary of useful German–English travel words and phrases.

PLACES TO STAY

There is no shortage of good places to stay in Mayrhofen and the Zillertal, as the whole district is geared to tourism and catering for visitors.

Hotels

The hotels and guesthouses are more expensive in Mayrhofen than those in the surrounding local villages, so if you are not bothered about night-life, you will find good bargains in the villages of Fuegen, Kaltenbach, Zell am Ziller and Ramsau. See Appendix A for a list of recommended accommodation in Mayrhofen and the Zillertal.

In Mayrhofen, the main centre of the Zillertal, hotels tend to cater for the tourist trade, but there is an abundance of guest houses and small hotels where climbers and walkers will feel more at home. And when booking huts over the internet, you will discover many huts have family connections with guest houses and hotels in the valley which they will be happy to recommend.

Youth hostels (Verein Volkshaus)

There are no youth hostels in Mayrhofen; the nearest hostel-style hotel is the Wurm-Ferienhof Bonholz, located 3km from the Kaltenbach-Stumm Zillertalbahn railway station, above the adjacent village of Stumm at Stummerberg.

Looking south along the Stilluppgrund valley on the Zillertal Rucksack Route (Stage 2)

- **Jugendherberge Wurm-Ferienhof Bonholz**, Stummerberg 68, A-6276 Stummerberg, tel 0043 5283 2959 991 or email jugendherberge-bonholz@gmx. at, www.jugendherberge-wurm.at

Innsbruck, which is the access point for the Peter Habeler Runde and the Zillertal South Tirol Tour, has three youth-hostel-type hotels reasonably close to the railway station and the tourist part of the city. You can check their availability by visiting www. jungehotels.at

- **Jugendherberge Fritz-Prior-Schwedenhaus**, Rennweg 17b, A-6020 Innsbruck – located in the district of Saggen by the River Inn (tel 0043 512 5858 1427 or email info@hostel-innsbruck.com, www.hostel-innsbruck.com)

- **Volkshaus Hostel Innsbruck**, Radetzky Strasse 47, A-6020 Innsbruck – located in the district of Reichenau (tel 0043 664 266 7004 or email info@hostel-innsbruck.at, www.hostel-innsbruck.at)

- **Jugendherberge Innsbruck and Studentenheim**, Reichenauer Strasse 147, A-6020 Innsbruck – located to the north-east of the city in the district of Reichenau, by the River Inn (tel 0043 512 346179/346180 or email info@youth-hostel-innsbruck.at, www.youth-hostel-innsbruck.at)

Campsites

For those travelling by road who wish to camp, good sites can be found at Schlitters on the outskirts of Mayrhofen (**Camping Kroell**, tel 0043

5285 62580), at Kaltenbach (**Camping Hochzillertal**, tel 0043 6507 333398), at Zell am Ziller (**Campingdorf Hofer**, tel 0043 5282 2248) and at Laubichl. See www.alpenparadies.com

Groups intending to camp should enquire from the campsite warden about reduced fees while they are away; this is referred to as *leeres zelt* (empty tent).

LOCAL TRANSPORT

Summer bus services

The following times are for the local Postbus service (so called because it also used to deliver the post), which leaves from Mayrhofen's combined train and bus station. Note, be sure to check online timetables before making any plans.

- **Mayrhofen to Ginzling/ Breitlahner/Schlegeis 4102:** 06: 40/07:35/08:35/09:05/09:35/10: 05/10:36/12:36/13:35/15:05/16: 36/17:05/18:10
- **Schlegeis to Mayrhofen:** 08:40/0 9:40/10:10/10:40/11:10/12:40/1 3:40/14:40/15:10/15:40/16:10/1 6:40/17:40/18:10
- **Breitlahner to Mayrhofen:** 08:55 /09:55/10:25/10:55/11:25/11:55/ 12:55/13:55/14:55/15:25/15:55/ 16:25/16:55/17:55/18:25
- **Ginzling to Mayrhofen:** 08:59/09 :59/10:29/10:59/11:29/11:59/12: 59/13:59/14:59/15:29/15:59/16: 29/16:59/17:59/18:29

Taxi services

For participants in groups, it can be more cost effective and convenient to make use of local Mayrhofen taxi services:

- **Taxi Kroell**, tel 0043 5285 62260 or email info@taxikroell.com
- **Taxi Reinis**, tel 0043 650 463 7575 or email reinis-taxi@aon.at
- **Taxi Thaler**, tel 0043 5285 634 23 or 0043 664 200 6596
- **Floitentaxi**, tel 0043 664 102 9354

Shuttle minibus service from Mayrhofen to Gruene Wand Haus

The shuttle service to Gruene Wand Haus takes 40min to make the 16km journey and leaves the Europahaus tourist information centre at the following times: 08:00/08:30/10:00/11:30/15:00; return service: 10:00/11:30/16:00.

To reserve the shuttle service, tel 0043 5285 634 23 or 0664 2006 596.

For the South Tirol at Pfitscherjochhaus, use Mietwagen Steiner for getting to and from Gasthof Stein from Pfitscherjoch (tel 0039 472 630 121 or mobile 0039 340 145 6313).

LOCAL SERVICES

Tourist offices

The main tourist information office and conference centre, the Europahaus, is located a five-minute walk from the railway station on

Durster Strasse. There are also satellite tourist offices in the town. See Appendix A for full contact details.

There is also an information centre at Naturparkhaus in Ginzling.

Post office and mail
The post office in Mayrhofen is located just off the main street in the centre of town and has fax, internet and money-exchange facilities. The post office is open Monday to Friday from 08:00 to 12:00 noon and from 14:00 to 18:00.

Post to Austria usually takes about five days. Postcards can be purchased at the huts and mailed from the hut's post box. The mail is taken down to the valley, usually once a week, and deposited at the main post office. Not surprisingly, post to the UK will take 10 to 20 days.

Places to leave luggage
There is a left-luggage facility at Mayrhofen's combined bus and railway station, which is open Monday to Saturday 08:00 to 18:00. Alternatively, should you be staying at one of the hotels, most hoteliers are quite happy to store luggage until you return.

PETER HABELER'S OFFICE (MOUNTAIN GUIDES)

Should you require the services of a professional mountain guide, these can be hired via Peter Habeler's Office on the *Haupt Strasse* (high street).

See Appendix A for more information or contact www.bergfuehrer-zillertal.at.

CHILDREN

I have been asked many times about the suitability of hut-to-hut touring for children. Most children I know or have met love visiting the various huts and the sense of freedom it bestows on them. The Austrian Alpine Club also actively encourages children to participate in mountain activities.

My own daughter traversed the entire length of the Rucksack Route and climbed several peaks along the way when she was 14 years old. I also know of nine- and ten-year-olds who have undertaken the majority of the tour without the Edel/Kasseler and Friesenberg/Gams hut connections.

If children are capable of ascending Ben Nevis, Snowdon or the round of Helvellyn, they will surely enjoy some of these tours. But only parents can decide, as some of the day's outings are quite long, particularly the Greizer to Berliner Hut and Berliner Hut to Furtschaglhaus connections. Children need to be fit, happy to be in the mountains for long periods of time and easily entertained, i.e., enjoy reading books, playing scrabble or simply chit-chatting. However, the best solution is to bring a friend with them for company and allow adequate stops and rest days.

Difficult ground at the Schoenbichlerscharte (ZRR, Stage 5)

THE AUSTRIAN ALPINE CLUB OEAV

(Oesterreichischer Alpenverein, founded 1862)

Huts throughout the Zillertal are administered by the Austrian and German Alpine Clubs, the OeAV and DAV, respectively, except those in the South Tirol, which are owned and administered by the Italian Alpine Club (CAI) or its regional equivalent, the Alpenverein Suedtirol (AVS).

The Oesterreichischer Alpenverein OeAV, which translates as the Austrian Alpine Association, was founded in 1862 to foster and encourage the sport of mountaineering. Its founding is largely credited to Franz Senn, who was the village priest in Neustift (Stubai valley) until his untimely death from pneumonia aged 52, and his associates Johann Studl, a wealthy Prague business man, and Karl Hofmann, a young lawyer from Munich.

Celebrating its 160th year anniversary in 2022, the Alpenverein was the first alpine club to be established in mainland Europe. Presently, the club has just over 650,000 members in 197 *Sektions* (sections) that embrace all facets of mountaineering. Membership is open to any person, without exception, who has a love of the mountains, regardless of age or ability.

The club's principal activities include developing mountain huts, marking and maintaining footpaths, producing maps, organising mountaineering courses and tackling environmental issues, particularly those which are seen to spoil the aesthetic appeal of the mountains, such as littering or inappropriate signage and graffiti.

The establishment of the UK section, OeAV Sektion Britannia, is largely credited to Major Walter Ingham and Henry Crowther, who both had strong links with Austria. Walter, while a UK citizen, spent many years in Vienna, including several years with the Control Commission just after World War 2. Henry was born Heinrich Kraus and came from the eastern city of Graz. He changed his name to the more English-sounding name of Henry when he became a naturalised British citizen. The UK Sektion of the OeAV was formed in 1948, just after World War 2, to foster Anglo-Austrian relationships between like-minded people in the spirit of mountaineering and to make it easier for British mountaineers in the immediate post-war years to visit the Eastern Alps.

Presently, OeAV Sektion Britannia is one of the largest UK mountaineering clubs, with over 13,000 members, ranking 12th in the Alpenverein as a whole. The Club organises its own activities, having a regular programme of indoor and outdoor meets; it also has its own website (see www.alpenverein.at/britannia) and produces a quarterly newsletter. The Club also runs training courses for its members, both in the UK and in Austria, through the Alpenverein Akademie mountaineering school. The Austrian Alpine Club (UK) enjoys full reciprocal rights agreements with all other alpine clubs: in France (CAF), Switzerland (CAS), Italy (CAI) and Germany (DAV). This means that should you cross into the South Tirol while in the Zillertal to stay at the Schwarzenstein Hut, for instance, you will pay the same fees as those enjoyed by members of the Italian Alpine Club and vice versa.

Anyone intending to undertake a hut-to-hut tour anywhere in Austria is strongly recommended to join OeAV Alpenverein Britannia. Apart from the real benefit of enjoying preferential treatment and reduced costs at the huts, perhaps the main advantage of being a member is that of belonging; this feeling of friendliness is greatly cherished and fostered by everyone and will be experienced many times when visiting various huts, particularly over a number of years. This is referred to as *Gemutlich* (homely).

Membership of the Austrian Alpine Club is, as previously noted, open to all regardless of age or ability and is recommended for everyone wishing to avail themselves of the benefits of reduced hut rates and the provision of mountain rescue insurance. There are different categories for adults, seniors, juniors, juveniles, children and family groups. Membership is renewed annually.

On acceptance of membership, the Club provides an internet link packed full of useful information: www.alpenverein.at/britannia/membership/member-benefits.php. See Appendix A for full contact details.

HUTS

The word 'hut' is a misnomer, as all the huts in the Zillertal, as described here, are more akin to mountain inns or guest houses, providing overnight accommodation and some form of restaurant service. For the mountain traveller, this means you do not have to return to the valley every few days to stock up on provisions.

Collectively, there are well over 1000 huts in Austria, half of which are owned by the Austrian and German Alpine Clubs. In the Zillertal there are a total of 30 OeAV and DAV huts, most of which are open from the end of June to mid September. All the huts in the Zillertal have a *Huettenwirt* (hut guardian), traditionally a *Bergfuehrer* (mountain guide), and his family. Each hut has simple sleeping accommodation in the form of a *Matratzenlager* (mixed dormitory) with blankets and pillows and a small number of *Bettzimmer* (bedrooms) with duvets and sheets.

In addition to sleeping accommodation, each hut will have some form of restaurant service offering a number of traditional dishes (see Appendix B). The menu generally comprises *Bergsteigeressen* (mountaineer food): soup, a choice of main meals, cold meats, cheese and sometimes cakes and sweets. All huts serve tea, coffee, beer, wine and so forth, and most huts will have a small shop where visitors can buy postcards, chocolate and biscuits.

On arrival at the hut, you should first remove your boots and store them

The historic 'ladies' room' at the Berliner Hut (ZRR Stages 4/4A, ZSTT Stage 7)

in the boot rack, which will be close to the front door. You should also hang your ice axe, crampons, rope and other clobber on the racks provided because such paraphernalia is not permitted in the dormitories and bedrooms. If you are wet on arrival, your waterproofs should be shaken as dry as possible outside and hung up to dry with your ice tackle. If you are in a group, do not mill around the doorway, and make sure your group leaves its surplus water and as much dirt off boots outside as possible. Many of the huts are spotlessly clean and, for the benefit of all guests, like to remain that way.

You should then establish contact with the *Huettenwirt* to obtain your overnight accommodation. (A maximum of three nights is the Club rule but, generally, this is not rigidly enforced.) You will usually find this most important person in the *Kuche* (kitchen), *Gastestube* (dining room) or *Bureau* (office).

Having found the *Huettenwirt* it is important to greet him or her by saying *Gruss Gott* (good day) and introduce yourself. Mention if you and your group are members of OeAV Alpenverein Britannia of the Austrian Alpine Club (or another alpine club) and tell them that you would like some accommodation. (Note, it is advisable to book ahead to ensure there is a room available.) The *Huettenwirt* is then likely to ask for your membership card(s), which may be retained overnight or until your departure, when you will be asked to pay.

If you do not speak German and feel uncomfortable attempting to ask for rooms in German, write down the following phrase: *Ich/wir hatte(n) gern ein Zimmer oder Matratzenlager, bitte* (I/we would like a room or dormitory, please). Be polite and always use *bitte* (please) and *danke* (thank you). Trivial as this may seem, these polite gestures are extremely important and will go a long way to ensuring a pleasant stay.

Should the hut be full, you may have to take up residence in the *Winterraum* (winter room), which is usually the reserve of ski mountaineers and those visiting when the hut is closed. The winter room is generally an annexe to the hut and may double as a storeroom or shelter for animals, as is the case at the Greizer Hut. While the winter room can be quite cosy, remember to keep your gear off the floor, as it is usually the home of the huts more permanent four-pawed furry residents.

Should the hut be beyond full, you will be provided with a mattress for *Notlager*, which roughly translates as 'sleeping with the furniture', be it on the floor, in the corridors, on tables, on benches or simply anywhere you can lie down.

Only on very rare occasions will you be asked to move on by the *Huettenwirt* and only when bed space has been secured at an adjacent hut and only when there is sufficient daylight for you to reach your destination. In the Zillertal this is a rare scenario, however, which means your only option would be the cosy but somewhat noisy situation of *Notlager*.

At the hut you will also require a *Schlafsack* (sheet sleeping bag) for use with the blankets and bedding provided by the hut; this is to minimise the amount of washing required and, subsequently, reduce water pollution downstream of the hut. Note this is a compulsory requirement. If you do not have one it is possible to hire one from the *Huettenwirt*.

You will also require a pair of hut shoes to wander around the hut, as many OeAV huts do not provide them. Boots upstairs is strictly *Verboten* (forbidden).

Each hut will have some form of male and female washrooms and toilet facilities, which vary from being excellent at the Berliner and Olperer Huts to being more modest at the Friesenberghaus and Greizer Hut.

However, it is likely that the provision of hot water at some huts will gradually diminish as the Club moves towards more simple and basic necessities to minimise its use of fuel and water.

Elsewhere in the hut, usually near the front door, you will find the *Trockenraum* (drying room), where wet clothes can be dried.

Thereafter, the heart and soul of the hut is the *Gastestube* (dining room). Here you will find all manner of activities going on: groups planning their next day, people celebrating a climb or a birthday, or people just chatting. The atmosphere is best described as *Gemutlichkeit*, which means homely and friendly, an ambience that is fostered and cherished throughout the whole of Austria.

At the end of your stay, remember to make your bed, fold your blankets and check you haven't forgotten anything. Search out the *Huettenwirt* and thank him/her and the staff for a pleasant stay. Remember to collect your membership card if it has not already been given back to you. Finally, fill in the hut book to record your stay and indicate where you are going next.

Hut reservations

Even if you are travelling solo, it is recommended that you contact the hut, either by phone or email prior to your arrival, more so if you are travelling as a group, as all the huts on the Hoehenweg get very busy, particularly at weekends and during the peak holiday season in August.

If you are travelling as a group, it is also recommended that you make your reservations early, making enquiries up to six months before your intended visit. Don't leave it too late as you will find the smaller huts will be fully booked.

Most of the huts in the Zillertal now have websites and email addresses, which makes it easier than ever to get in touch directly and make a reservation online. There is also an attempt by the OeAV, DAV and AVS to rationalise various online hut

Be prepared for unseasonable weather

reservation practices into one amalgamated platform that will allow individuals and groups to make hut reservations and payments at a one-stop shop via the internet. See www.alpenverein.at/huetten, www.alpsonline.org/guest/login. See 'Hut directory' also for details.

It is also possible to make a block booking of all the huts on the Zillertal Rucksack Route and the Peter Habeler Runde by contacting the Naturparkhaus tourist office in Ginzling (tel 0043 5286 52181 or email info@naturpark-zillertal.at, www.naturpark-zillertal.at).

Having made your reservation, remember to reconfirm your booking directly with the hut just before you travel and again by phone the day before your visit, to let them know you're on your way and will turn up.

Reservation cancellations

Because of the ease with which huts can now be booked over the internet and by phone, abuse of this facility is beginning to become an issue, particularly when reservations are made and folk do not turn up; this results in not only a loss of business for the huts but also in a significant waste of food. Some huts are now asking for deposits to offset some of this risk. Note that in Austrian law, if you make a reservation and do not cancel in adequate time, you are still liable for the full costs, or part of, incurred by the hut. Most huts are businesses, and it is only polite that should you have to cancel your reservation, you make every effort to do so – if not, don't be surprised if you receive a bill!

Hut descriptions and locations

Huts throughout the Zillertal are administered by the Austrian and German Alpine Clubs, the OeAV and DAV, respectively, except for those that are privately owned, and those in the South Tirol, which are owned and administered by the Italian Alpine Club, the CAI, or Alpenverein Suedtirol, the AVS.

As more of the huts in the Zillertal introduce websites and email addresses, readers can book online and access the most up-to-date information on the huts.

For more information see the 'Hut directory' later in this guide and Appendix A for websites and other useful information.

HUT MEALS AND MENUS

All huts have some sort of restaurant service to cover the three daily meals: *Fruehstuck* (breakfast), *Mittagessen* (lunch) and *Abendessen* (dinner). Tea, coffee, hot chocolate, lemonade, cola, beer, wine and schnapps are all available at the huts. Drinks are served in *Viertel* (quarter) or *Halbe* (half) litres or in *gross* (large) or *klein* (small) and maybe *heiss* (hot) or *kalt* (cold).

Breakfast is served from approximately 06:00 to 07:30. Thereafter, no meals are available until lunchtime because the hut staff are busy with general housekeeping. Breakfast is seen as the worst value for money, but unless you are carrying your own provisions you will have little choice other than to accept it. Breakfast usually comprises two or three slices of bread; a portion of butter, jam and cheese; and a choice of tea or coffee. If you do not finish it, take it with you as you pay for it all.

Lunch and dinner are the main meals of the day and are served with a selection of vegetables or salad; *Vegetarische* (vegetarian) options will also be available.

Lunchtime is usually from 12:00 to 14:00 but varies from hut to hut. However, it is possible to purchase simple meals, such as *Suppe* (soup), *Kaese Brot* (cheese bread), *Apfelstrudl* (apple strudel), at most of the huts throughout the afternoon.

Dinner is the main meal of the day and is generally served from 18:00 to 19:30. Apart from meals listed on the menu, *Bergsteigeressen* will also be available. Literally translated, it means 'mountain climbers' food' and in reality that is what it is – even if it is potluck what you get. However, it is a low-priced meal and must contain a minimum of 500 calories. The meal generally comprises spaghetti or other pasta, potatoes, some meat or sausage, sometimes a fried egg or maybe a dumpling. There is no hard and fast rule other than that it is relatively inexpensive and there is usually a lot of it.

Appendix B lists many of the items found on a typical hut *Speisekarte* (menu), as well as some useful words and phrases for when ordering food and drink.

Meals and menus

Speisekarte

Gerstelsuppe mit oder ohne Wurst	Käsenocken mit Krautsalat
Gulaschsuppe	Spinatknödel mit Krautsalat
Knödelsuppe	Hochfeilermix
Leberknödelsuppe	Röstkartoffel + Eier + Speck
Spaghetti	Röstkartoffel + Eier + Leberkäs
Wienerschnitzel mit Beilagen	Kaiserschmarren Kompott oder Preiselbeeren
Naturschnitzel mit Beilagen	Apfelstrudel

Bergsteigeressen

Generally, before ordering meals, you must first organise a table. There is no formality, but sometimes groups of tables may be marked *privat* (private) or *Reservierung* (reservation) when mountaineering training courses are being run. Once you have sat down, one of the *Kellnerinnen* (waitresses) will take your order. Alternatively, you may have to go to the counter or *Kueche* (kitchen) to order, or there may be a sign marked *Selbstbedienung*, which means self-service.

The general rule for paying for food and drink is by way of an accumulative bill. Therefore, visitors are advised to note their consumption to aid checking at the time of paying. Take note, these bills/lists can be considerable when staying at a hut for more than a couple of nights.

As a guideline for working out a budget, typical meal costs can be equated to similar prices for a decent bar meal plus drinks in most British pubs. The half-board cost is currently €55–65, depending on the category of the hut.

Because of the excellent service the huts provide, there is little need to carry your own food. However, many people bring their own dry rations: tea, coffee, bread, cheese, etc. This allows you to make your own snacks, and by borrowing cups and purchasing *ein Liter Teewasser* (a litre of water for tea), you can brew up at a small cost.

The only facility not provided for is self-catering, and it does seem a little pointless when all the meals are reasonably priced.

KIT LIST

In terms of how much kit to take, the following is a good rule of thumb: one on, one off and the odd spare.

When travelling as a group, try to share items that have a commonality of equipment to minimise each person's weight. For example, you will only need one comprehensive first-aid kit, one repair kit, one set of maps, one guidebook, one phrase book, one pair of binoculars and one set of spare batteries if all the headlamps are the same.

- Rucksack (50 litre)
- Boots (suitable for all seasons)
- Trekking poles (optional)
- Socks x 2 pairs
- Trousers
- Shorts (optional)
- Underwear x 3
- Shirts x 2
- Light fleece pullover
- Light windproof jacket
- Waterproofs: jacket and trousers
- Hat and gloves
- Gaiters (optional)
- Headlamp-cum-torch
- Toiletries plus pack towel
- Water bottle or thermos flask
- First-aid kit with suncream and lip salve
- Sunglasses plus spare pair
- Repair kit: needle and thread, super glue, candle, binding wire
- Pocket knife

Alpine walking skills – essential kit: good four-season boots, trekking poles, microspikes, 2.4m sling and jumbo karabiner for improvised harness

- Selection of polythene bags
- Maps and compass
- Whistle
- Notepad and pencil

- Zillertal guide book – that is, this one!
- Emergency gear, bivvy bag, food rations

- Personal optional items, such as German phrase book, camera, binoculars
- Hut wear: a lightweight change of clothes, hut shoes or socks, trousers, shirt, sheet sleeping bag and inflatable pillow

Also recommended for walkers: a set of microspikes and a 2.4m-long x 10mm-wide Dyneema tape sling with a large jumbo-sized screwgate karabiner.

Should you intend to climb some of the peaks, you will need to add the following to the above list – and know how to use them:

- Ice axe
- Crampons
- 2 x large slings with screwgate karabiners

- 3 x Prussik loops
- Harness
- Ice screw
- 2 x spare karabiners
- A length of rope, such as 50m x 9mm, for each group of three people
- Also a few odds and ends, such as a small selection of slings with nuts, a pulley, a universal rock piton

For crevasse rescue you will generally need five karabiners at your disposal.

The following items are also useful within a group: altimeter, ice hammer, deadman or other snow anchor belay device and Prussiking devices, such as a Petzl Tibloc or Wild Country Ropeman.

Old Gothic sign

Typical rock sign

ROUTE FINDING

Paths throughout the Zillertal are way-marked roughly every hundred metres or so with a daub of red paint.

At intersections, paths frequently have a signpost or, alternatively, a red-and-white paint marker with a designated path number; this in turn is cross-referenced to maps and guide-books, including this one.

Paths throughout, such as on the Zillertal Rucksack Route, vary from traditional mountain paths to tracks across boulder fields and rough ground. Participants will also encounter steep ground, late-summer snow and fixed wire ropes here and there, which have been installed to aid your stability.

Paths for hut-to-hut routes are frequently marked with a signpost just outside the hut; they give the standard time in hours to travel between the huts without stops and a colour code difficulty grade of blue, red or black mountain trails.

Routes onto and across glaciers are by definition black mountain trails and for the experienced only because tracks onto and across glaciers are not normally marked, as the route can vary from year to year. Also, if venturing onto glaciers, you are expected to have the necessary know-how and route-finding skills plus the necessary equipment. However, sometimes local guides will place marker poles on the glacier to aid route finding, such as those on the heavily crevassed Floiten Kees glacier.

Where the route description refers to the left or right bank of a river, stream or glacier, this is when viewed in the direction of flow; this means that

Negotiating ladders over old moraines at the foot of the Schwarzensteinkees glacier (ZSTT Stage 7)

in ascent the left bank will be on your right. To avoid confusion, efforts have been made throughout the text to add a compass bearing to ensure participants go in the right direction.

Given the above, no great demand will be made on the individual's route-finding skills, except on routes noted in the text as having the odd navigational difficulty.

Map makers have also endeavoured to enable better route interpretation by providing different types of path markings: solid red lines for easy trails, dashed red lines for footpaths and dotted red lines for narrow steep paths; supporting symbols have been added to show fixed wires and ladders.

However, as with all mountains, the Zillertal included, route finding is made much more difficult in mist, rain and snow.

While the information provided is as accurate as possible, this may change from year to year due to landslips, avalanches and erosion.

MAPS

The following maps are required for the Zillertal Rucksack Route. The maps are published by the Austrian Alpine Club and are available from the UK Section of the Austrian Alpine Club (UK).

Alpenvereinskarte Zillertaler Alpen
- Sheet 35/1 Westliches (West), Scale 1:25,000
- Sheet 35/2 Mitte (Central), Scale 1:25,000

Also recommended, since the maps cover the complete region at a glance and are available from major map retailers:
- **Freytag & Berndt Wanderkarte:** Sheet 152 Mayrhofen, Zillertal Alpen, Gerlos-Krimml, Scale 1:50,000
- **Kompass Wanderkarte:** Sheet 037 Mayrhofen, Tuxer Tal, Zillergrund, Scale 1:25,000 + smart app

Books
For guidebooks, websites and other reading, see Appendix C.

Alpenvereinaktiv App
The Alpenverein has also developed mapping software, Alpenvereinaktiv, for use on mobile phones and digital tablets, which can be accessed via Alpenvereinaktiv.com. The Alpenverein is keen to promote the use of Alpenvereinaktiv, first as a tour-planning tool and as a physical tool while undertaking a tour.

The Alpenvereinaktiv application offers three levels of access: the basic application is free and includes tour planning, height profiles, commentary and photos; this is followed by the Pro and Pro+ versions, which can be purchased as a monthly or annual subscription and include GPS tracking, 3D video and satellite photos.

Mountain terminology
See Appendix B for a glossary of German–English words that may be

useful when route finding and navigating in the Zillertal Alps.

ALPINE WALKING SKILLS

So, how do these skills differ in the Zillertal from walking elsewhere?

Put simply, and as mentioned in the route-grading segment, it's the variance in the terrain that makes Alpine walking different. On a single walk you may encounter easy paths, stone-covered tracks, large rocky boulder fields, paths with fixed wire ropes and the odd patch of hard-packed snow. Sometimes just the strength-sapping distances involved when carrying a touring rucksack can make Alpine walking far more of a challenge.

Boots: It is essential that you have a relatively stiff boot with good ankle support and a stout Vibram-type rubber sole. Many of the walks involve sustained hard walking over rocky slopes and glacial debris, plus encounters with patches of old hard snow. It is important to think of your boots as tools that can be used to kick steps and jam into rocky cracks without causing damage to your feet. While bendy boots may be a tad lighter and more comfortable, they are no match for a good pair of four-season mountaineering boots when it comes to dealing with difficult ground.

Microspikes: While crampons are normally associated with climbers, a pair of these little tools often comes in handy when the weather decides to dump some unseasonable snow

in July or August, and they may help provide you with a little extra security when you get up close to some old, hard-packed snow.

Improvised harness: Many of the routes are equipped with fixed wire ropes to provide some support over stretches of difficult terrain. While these may be relatively easy to cross, it is the consequences of a fall that should be borne in mind. Also, not everyone has a head for heights, and the use of an improvised harness will help provide confidence and security of passage. Constructed from a 2.4m-long by 10mm-wide Dyneema sling, three or four overhand knots and a large jumbo-sized screwgate karabiner, the sling will allow you to clip into those fixed wires whenever the need arises and arrest a fall when you least expect it.

These slings can also be daisy-chained together to provide a useful short rope should the need arise, provided everyone carries one.

Trekking poles: Almost standard accessories for most folk these days but in the Alps trekking poles come into their own, especially when crossing glacial steams and traversing steep patches of old snow.

GLACIERS AND GLACIER TRAVEL

The glaciers of the Zillertal Alps are in the heartland of the Eastern Alps. Quite a few of the mountaineering routes described in this guide, particularly on the Grosser Moeseler and the Schwarzenstein, involve crossing or negotiating glaciers over a period of several hours. It goes without saying that before committing to climbing these peaks, you should have the requisite skills and equipment to navigate such glacial terrain safely. Should this be your first foray into glacier territory, you are strongly advised to undertake some formal training beforehand.

The UK Section of the Austrian Alpine Club organises basic training in glacier crossing and crevasse rescue through the OeAV Alpenverein subsidiary WELDbewegend, the commercial arm of Alpenverein Edelweiss in Vienna. See www.alpenverein.at/britannia/activities/training.php or contact the AAC (UK) office for details aacuk.org.uk.

The National Outdoor Centre at Plas y Brenin in North Wales and Glenmore Lodge in Scotland also run similar introductory alpine skills courses where you can practise crevasse-rescue techniques from the safe, dry land of local crags and climbing walls. Contact www.pyb.co.uk and www.glenmorelodge.org.uk.

A further alternative is to hire a professional mountain guide for a day via British Mountain Guides www.bmg.org.uk.

A very informative DVD, *Alpine Essentials*, is also available from the British Mountaineering Council (BMC).

The motto is to practise before you go.

Knotted rope technique at the Schwarzensteinsattel (ZSTT Stage 7)

HEALTH AND SAFETY

While you do not have to be super fit to undertake these tours, it is essential that participants are used to walking for six hours continuously while carrying a touring-sized rucksack weighing in the region of 12–15kg.

Altitude

The average altitude experienced on the tour is in the region of 2500–3000m (8000–10,000ft). It is, therefore, not common for people visiting the Zillertal to suffer badly from altitude sickness.

However, that's not to say you won't feel the effects of altitude, such as feeling out of puff, a mild headache or slowed pace, particularly on the higher peaks of the Grosser Moeseler and the Olperer.

The best defence against altitude is to be as fit as possible, eat and drink normally and ensure you get adequate rest and sleep. However, should you experience symptoms that persist or worsen, it would be prudent to descend to a lower altitude.

Mountain rescue and personal insurance

The three tours detailed in this guide involve sustained activity in a high-mountain environment. Inevitably, this increases the risk of an accident taking place, such as a severe fall, breaking a limb or some other serious mishap, resulting in the mountain rescue team being called out.

As noted elsewhere, one of the benefits of membership of the OeAV is mountain rescue insurance in case

Difficult ground on the approach to the Floitenkees glacier; note the waymark sign on the rock (ZRR Stage 4)

of accidents. This can be supplemented by a specialist insurance company, details of which are available from the Austrian Alpine Club (UK) or by simply scanning the advertisement sections in one of the many climbing magazines. Similarly, the BMC has an excellent insurance policy, which can be obtained separately to membership.

The value of insurance should not be underestimated; the cost of a mountain rescue can be considerable when helicopters, police and professional mountain guides are brought into use, unlike in the UK, where mountain rescue services are generally provided free of charge by the local authority public services department and groups of enthusiastic volunteers. In the alpine regions most countries will charge the hapless victim. Be warned!

Mountain rescue is as much about prevention as it is about cure so before you go, please check all your gear and practise constructing your improvised, rudimentary harness as well as the time-consuming tasks of putting on crampons/harnesses and roping up. Most importantly, practise your crevasse-rescue techniques.

Global Health Insurance Card (GHIC)

This card, previously known as the EHIC and E111, is available free from any post office or online. To qualify for the card, you must be living legally in the UK; see www.nhs.uk for details of eligibility. Simply fill out the form and you will receive a credit-card-sized GHIC identity card, which entitles you to free medical care in any EU member state, in this case Austria. Should you be unfortunate to need medical attention while on holiday, this card will help you to pay your way.

However, the GHIC only entitles you to those services provided free in the member state; it does not cover any aspect of medical repatriation. In Mayrhofen the nearest hospital-clinic where the GHIC card is valid is the hospital (*Krankenhaus*) at Schwaz, not far from Innsbruck.

It is important that you still take out good personal travel insurance to supplement that provided by the GHIC.

Doctors

Should you need to visit a doctor or pharmacist, look out for the green cross sign that is usually displayed

Doctor's surgery sign

outside a general practioner's clinic. See Appendix A for further details and contacts.

Coronavirus pandemic (Covid 19)

As a result of the Coronavirus pandemic in 2020, many restrictions were put in place; many of these affected air, train and bus travel, but they also affected how hut accommodation operated. Post-Covid-19, some restrictions at huts may continue for the foreseeable, such as the availability of bedding, restrictions on group size, overnight provision by reservation only and confirmation of a negative lateral flow test on arrival. Hopefully, all restrictions will ease over time, but until such time as they do, check the latest guidelines before you go and it makes sense to have several lateral flow test kits as part of your first-aid kit.

Emergency phone numbers in Austria

The following numbers can be dialled from a mobile phone, even when the phone indicates there is no reception from your service provider. Fortunately, mobile phone reception is excellent in Austria.

It is worthwhile popping these numbers into your mobile phone, then you don't have to look them up should the need arise:

- Mountain rescue (*Bergrettung* Austria) 140
- Mountain rescue (*Bergrettung* Italy) 118
- Red Cross (*Rotes Kreutz*) 144
- European emergency phone number 112.

Helicopter rescue

Should you require a helicopter rescue:

- Remain at least 50 metres from the helicopter
- Do not approach the helicopter unless the winch man signals you to do so
- Do not approach the helicopter from behind
- Ensure that all loose items of equipment are made secure.

ELECTRONIC DEVICES

Folk who are wedded to and rely heavily on their mobile phone or tablet should note that the electrical infrastructure in most huts is, at best, extremely modest, with few if any places to recharge your phone, tablet or camera battery. Some huts have started to provide a common multi-gang terminal USB charging unit in dining rooms, but these tend to fill up quickly with devices when the hut is busy. It is recommended that you take with you (perhaps as part of a group kit) a portable USB battery pack and a twin or triple USB charging socket that allows you to extend any USB provision provided by the hut. For cameras, the best option is to take enough spare batteries with you for the length of the tour.

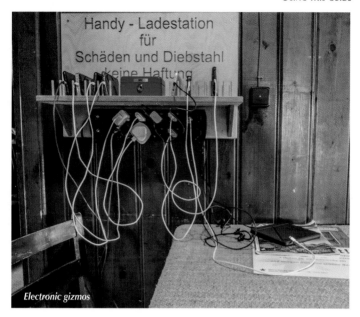

Electronic gizmos

USING THIS GUIDE

As previously mentioned, the routes described follow recognised paths and tracks corresponding to those indicted on maps and signposts.

However, to aid route finding across unfamiliar ground, each daily tour itinerary is fully described and illustrated with a map indicating the main topographical features that will be observed en route.

Route grading

The routes described are for people who are already involved in some sort of mountain activity on a regular basis. The tours range from moderate to quite strenuous, and you will need to be able to carry a full rucksack for an average of six to seven hours a day. In terms of alpine grading, the majority of the routes fall into the mountaineering grade of easy to moderate, comprising sustained mountain walking and requiring the ability to negotiate steep ground, scramble over rocks, cross late-summer snow, make use of fixed wire ropes and have a good head for heights.

To help participants determine what they can expect to encounter on the popular routes between huts, the Alpenverein (OeAV and DAV) has devised a colour-coded system

At the Edel Hut (ZRR Stage 1)

for marking fingerpost signs, similar to the skiing grades of blue, red and black: blue being the easiest and black the hardest. The trekking grades are as follows:

- **Blue** – Routes on wide tracks within permanently settled regions in the forest. Prior mountain experience or special equipment is not required.

Mountain trails: Routes mostly above the timber/forest line. Basic alpine experience and knowledge are required. Mountain trails are divided into red and black trails, according to their level of difficulty.

- **Red mountain trails** – Narrow routes of intermediate difficulty with steep sections, secured footpaths (fixed wires/ropes) or short climbing sections (scrambling). Alpine experience, good physical shape, surefootedness and mountaineering equipment are required. See kit list for guidance.

- **Black mountain trails** – Very difficult, narrow paths with many steep sections and precipices, secured footpaths (fixed wires/ropes) and longer climbing sections (scrambling). Alpine experience, excellent stamina, surefootedness, a good head for heights and expert hiking equipment are absolutely essential. See kit list for guidance.

Most of the trekking/hiking described in this guidebook follows red and black routes and blue approach routes.

The ascents of the peaks are all graded mountaineering routes; they range from easy peaks of alpine grade Facile (F), no significant difficulties, such as the Hoher Riffler, to moderately difficult peaks of alpine grade Peu Difficile (PD), good mountaineering skills required, such as the Grosser Moeseler and the Olperer, which have a number of short rather than sustained difficulties.

Standard times

At the beginning of each route description a standard time in hours is given as an estimate of the time required to walk from hut to hut. This time is generally on the generous side compared with those given by the Alpenverein, the huts themselves and the times given on the route direction signs. The time stated is the number of hours spent on the move and does not include lunch stops and other breaks. Most British parties find it difficult to attain the Alpenverein times. Be advised that this is of no consequence, as a good number of the quoted times are unattainable and seem to have been set by very fit athletes. With this in mind, the route descriptions in this book quote the actual time required when carrying a heavy touring rucksack.

On the excursion to climb Ahornspitze (ZRR)

At the Olperer Hut, looking towards Schlegeis and the peaks of the Grosser Moseler left and Hochfeiler right (ZRR Stage 7)

If in doubt, you can always work out an approximate time yourself by adding the sum of 20 minutes per kilometre and one hour per 300m of ascent.

Participants undertaking the tour with children are advised to add at least one hour to the standard time to allow for frequent picnic stops. Similarly, aspiring alpinists should make due allowance to the standard time while they learn the rudiments of glacier travel and the time-consuming activity of roping up and adding and removing crampons.

Spellings

You may well encounter discrepancies in the spelling of place names between those used in this book and those found on signposts, in the huts and on maps.

This is an issue across German-speaking countries which use the *Eszett*, ß, and umlauts on the 'ö' and the 'ü'. In practice, this shouldn't cause confusion as long as travellers are aware of it. In this guidebook the *Eszett* is presented as a double 's', as in *weiss*, and umlauts are presented as 'oe' or 'ue', as appropriate.

ZILLERTAL RUCKSACK ROUTE

Difficult ground leading to the footbridge and approach to the Garberkar (ZRR Stage 5)

TREK 1

Zillertal Rucksack Route

Start	Mayrhofen
Finish	Mayrhofen
Distance	79.5km
Ascent	6445m
Descent	8500m
Time	9 days
Excursions	Ahornspitze, Wollbachspitze, Gruene Wand Spitze, Grosser Loeffler, Berliner Spitze, Grosser Moeseler, Olperer, Hoher Riffler, Peterskoepfl, Vordere Grinbergspitze

At this stage it is important to offer some clarification about the different names of the Zillertal Rucksack Route and describe the various stages of development it has undertaken over many years before becoming the fine tour that we know today. In this guidebook, the tour is referred to by its original English name, the Zillertal Rucksack Route, which it was given immediately after World War 2 as a simple description of what was required to complete the route: nothing more than a rucksack and pair of boots. The tour is variously described in German as the Berliner Hoehenweg (Berliner High-Level Way) or the Zillertaler Runde Tour (Zillertal Round Tour).

If you were to ask Cicerone to recommend a muliti-day trek in the Alps with each day passing through a stunning mountain scenery of peaks, passes and glaciers, then the Zillertal Alps would definitely be on the list. The stunning array of snow-capped peaks and some of the best huts in the Alps make the Zillertal Alps one of the most prized regions of the Eastern Alps.

The original route of the early 1900s comprised only the Greizer, Berliner and Furtschaglhaus hut connections. The Kasseler–Greizer Hut connection was added around 1930, with limited access via the Stilluptal valley.

Over the next 30 years, the route remained virtually unchanged and it was not until the late 1960s and early 1970s that it saw significant development as a spin-off from a hydroelectricity project, which led to improved access up all of the side valleys through the construction of service roads used to build the reservoirs. Later, around 1977, the route was completed when various hunting paths around the high alms were linked together and cleared of vegetation.

A review of the route summary table will determine your confidence to do the full round. While the stages are long in distance and duration, they are not overly demanding. Providing you plan for this, and the weather is good, you should be fine. If you have children with you, you will need to err on the side of caution. Perhaps the best option for a family group would be to start at the Kasseler Hut (see route description under Kasseler Hut) and end at the Friesenberghaus. An ascent of the Ahornspitze can be undertaken as a day trip from Mayrhofen.

The length of the tour is 79 to 88km, depending on where you start and finish, and it ascends some 6700m.

Approaching the Greizer Hut (bottom right), looking towards the Floitenkees glacier and the Trippachsattel to Italy and the South Tirol (ZRR Stage 3)

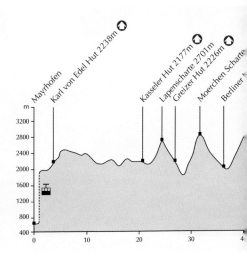

The route can be followed in either direction, although the clockwise course, as described here, is seen as being moderately easier and the preferred start due to the proximity of the Edel Hut to Mayrhofen.

Gruss Gott und Sehr Gut Zillertal Berg Touren

- Stage 1 Mayrhofen to Karl von Edel Hut 3hr
- *Excursion: Ascent of Ahornspitze (2973m) ascent 2–2½hr, descent 1–1½hr*
- Stage 2 Karl von Edel Hut to Kasseler Hut 8–10hr
- *Excursion: Ascent of Wollbachspitze (3210m) ascent 4hr, descent 3hr*
- *Excursion: Ascent of Gruene Wand Spitze (2946m) ascent 3hr, descent 2¼*
- Stage 3 Kasseler Hut to Greizer Hut 6–7hr
- *Excursion: Ascent of Grosser Loeffler (3379m) ascent 5hr, descent 4hr*
- Stage 4 Main route: Greizer Hut to Berliner Hut 6–8hr
- Stage 4A Greizer Hut to Berliner Hut via Schwarzenstein Hut 8–10hr

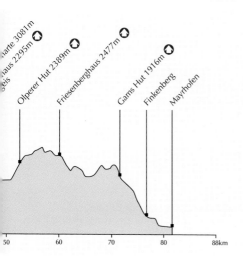

- *Excursion: Ascent of Berliner Spitze (3254m) ascent 4–5hr, descent 3–4hr*
- Stage 5 Berliner Hut to Furtschaglhaus 7–8hr
- *Excursion: Ascent of Grosser Moeseler (3480m) ascent 4–5hr, descent 3–4hr*
- Stage 6 Furtschaglhaus to Olperer Hut 5–6hr
- Stage 6A Furtschaglhaus to Olperer Hut via Pfitscherjochhaus 2 days
- *Excursion: Ascent of Olperer (3476m) ascent 4–5hr, descent 3hr*
- Stage 7 Olperer Hut to Friesenberghaus 2½–3hr
- *Excursion: Ascent of Hoher Riffler (3168m) ascent 3hr, descent 2½*
- *Excursion: Ascent of Peterskoepfl (2677m) ascent ¾hr, descent ½hr*
- Stage 8 Friesenberghaus to Gams Hut 10–12hr
- *Excursion: Ascent of Vordere Grinbergspitze (2765m) ascent 3hr, descent 1½hr*
- Stage 9 Gams Hut to Ginzling and Mayrhofen 3hr
- Stage 9A Gams Hut to Finkenberg and Mayrhofen 2hr

STAGE 1
Mayrhofen to Karl von Edel Hut

Start	Mayrhofen (632m)
Finish	Karl von Edel Hut (2238m)
Distance	4km
Ascent	285m
Descent	Negligible
Standard time	About 3hr from Mayrhofen

A pleasant introductory walk to the Zillertal Rucksack Route.

From Mayrhofen's combined Zillertalbahn railway station and bus terminus, cross the main road and turn right, heading S up the main road into Mayrhofen. After approximately 200 metres, turn left before a garage-cum-filling-station, following the road to the town centre and passing the very grand Elisabeth Hotel on the right-hand side and Mayrhofen's main post office a little further on.

From the post office, turn right at the road junction and continue the urban walk uphill for around 15min, passing lots of shops and expensive-looking places until you reach the Penkenbahn cable-car station on the right-hand side. Pass this and continue up the high street to a bridge across the river. Turn left just after the bridge and follow signposts for the Ahornbahn/Filzenboden cable car, which you will reach after a further 5min.

En route on the *Hauptstrasse* (main street) you will pass the alpine school and mountain guides office owned by legendary Austrian mountaineer **Peter Habeler**. Peter, with Reinhold Messner from the South Tirol, took the then mountaineering world by storm with many audacious ascents, including the first oxygen-free ascent of Mount Everest. However,

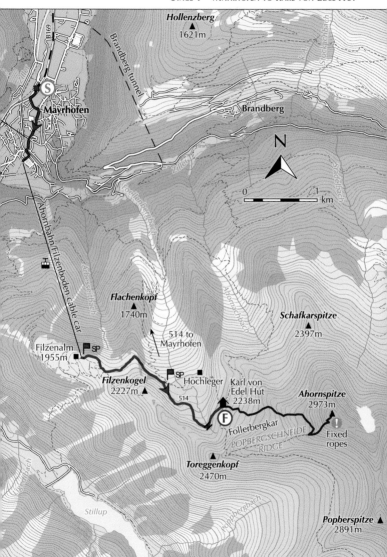

their skill is best summed up by their 10-hour ascent of the North face of the Eiger at a time when even the most competent of climbers would take at least two days.

Meanwhile, at our modest level, when purchasing your ticket remember the all-important *Gruss Gott* (good day) and ask for *einfach bitte* (one-way ticket). Show your OeAV membership card to obtain a modest discount.

The cable-car ride takes around 5min and provides excellent views across Mayrhofen as you are whisked high above the Zillertal valley in a cable car that boasts of being the largest in the Tirol and is akin to a double-decker bus laid flat on its side.

Banners of the DAV and Tirol at the Karl von Edel Hut

From the upper cable-car station and restaurant at **Filzenalm** (1955m), proceed onto the grassy terrace, past

the children's adventure park, and follow signs for Route 514 and the Edel Hut.

The route follows a well-marked path E, then SE around the jagged ridge of the Filzenschneide into a rock garden with boulders of house-sized proportions from where the hut at the base of the west ridge of the Ahornspitze is clearly visible (signpost). **1hr** From this point forward, further description is not required, as in summer the trail is a very popular day's outing from Mayrhofen and is a much-frequented tourist route to the **Edel Hut**. 1½–2hr

EXCURSION
Ascent of Ahornspitze (2973m)

Start	Karl von Edel Hut (2238m)
Distance	3km
Ascent	735m
Grade	F
Standard time	Ascent 2–2½hr; descent 1–1½hr
Note	For map, see Stage 1

The problem for the Edel Hut is that it is, unfortunately, very much a one-mountain hut, unless you are a day-tripper from Mayrhofen or en route to the Kasseler Hut. That aside, the Ahornspitze is a fine mountain in its own right, offering something of a challenge on its upper slopes and with some of the finest panoramic views in the region.

Having dumped much of your gear at the hut, you can make a lightweight ascent as an afternoon excursion through the mountain's west flank via the Follenbergkar, which, roughly translated, means 'rocks and boulders fallen off the mountain'. It is otherwise a straightforward route up and down a popular mountain. Enjoy!

The route starts off following an old, well-marked trail E along a glacial moraine with signs along the way telling

There are great views here across the Stillupgrund valley towards the Kasseler Hut.

would-be climbers to *Weg am Blieb* (keep to the path). After about ¾hr you will reach a *Gesprutt* (route closed) sign blocking off the old path, which was obliterated by a rock avalanche in 2002, and directing you S across the stone-strewn couloir to a small but obvious col on the **Popbergschneide ridge**. **1¾hr** ◄ Be careful hereabouts as the ridge is very exposed.

From here on, follow the obvious rocky ridge E, with good scrambling here and there. It is very exposed in places and requires a good head for heights. After a short hour the ridge steepens considerably just below the rocks that form the true summit. The lower second summit is visible just 100 metres away. Descend the rocks into a gap (fixed wires) and scramble up once more to the large summit cross. **About ¾hr** (2½hr from the hut)

South summit of the Ahornspitze, with the snow-covered Schwarzenstein in the far distance

From the summit excellent **views** abound in all directions, especially to the south towards Mayrhofen and the long Zillertal valley. Elsewhere,

the snow-capped peaks are just a little too far away to provide any serious interest, apart from the Grosser Loeffler to the south and the Grossvenediger, the fourth highest peak in Austria, to the east. Closer at hand, Brandberger Kolm can be seen to the north-east. To the east is the Zillergrund reservoir, and finally those with sharp eyes, perhaps assisted by binoculars, will be able to locate the Plauener Hut and Reichenspitze.

From the summit descend via the same route, taking a little more care as you scramble down the steep rocks. Once at the little col, take time to recce the route to the Kasseler Hut, as the first part of the route along the Siebenschneidenweg around the Popbergkar couloir and boulder field is clearly obvious. **1–1½hr**

STAGE 2
Karl von Edel Hut to Kasseler Hut
_____

Start	Karl von Edel Hut (2238m)
Finish	Kasseler Hut (2177m)
Distance	12.5km
Ascent	750m
Descent	800m
Standard time	8–10hr

This is a fitting way to start the Zillertal Rucksack Route proper. Not for the faint hearted, this first-class, long-distance trail traverses the hillside high above the Stillupgrund valley, across challenging terrain and ever-changing scenery.

First established during the 1970s by members of the DAV Wuerzburg and Aschaffenburger Sektions, and not surprisingly named the Aschaffenburger Hoehensteig, the route is now more popularly known as the Siebenschneidenweg, the Seven Ridges Way.

Despite the warning sign, *Nur Fuer Geubte* (only for the experienced), outside the Edel Hut, which I am sure puts off a number of very capable groups, this is a very good long-distance walk. Although it is long, it will satisfy most enthusiasts as the length of the walk is a good measure of personal fitness. The route traverses high above the steeply sided valley of Stillupgrund, roughly on the 2300m contour line, and provides excellent scenery throughout its length.

Once past the little col of Popbergneider, just beyond the Edel Hut, your attention will be firmly fixed on the south, towards the splendid Grosser Loeffler (3379m) and across the valley to the sharp-pointed peak of Gigalitz and the obvious col of the Lapenscharte.

CAUTIONARY NOTES

The suggested time required for this walk is 10hr, which reflects advice given on the signs outside the Edel Hut; this comprises 8½hr for the journey, plus 1hr for stops and ½hr for any mishaps. Essentially, you need to be on your way no later than 06:00.

Arrange with the *Huettenwirt* for breakfast and thermos flasks to be left on the dining room tables for an early start.

The sign outside the hut warns that this is an extremely long walk and should only be undertaken in settled weather by experienced and properly equipped people. In the event of bad weather, the only escape routes are on the north side of the Nofertenschneide at the Sammerschartl, then later at Maderegg Alm, when it would be easier and safer to return to the Edel Hut than descend the very steep forest trails into Stillupgrund, which is made more complex by having to cross a number of difficult streams. Once past the Nofertensmauer rock wall, you are committed to completing the walk to the Kasseler Hut, although there is the added assurance of shelter at the Biwak Notunterkunft should you require it.

While the route is characterised by the crossing of seven ridges and spurs, it is crossing the many boulder fields and negotiating the fixed ropes and steep grassy slopes that absorbs time and saps your concentration.

Should the weather be against you, you can always miss out this section by going straight to the Kasseler Hut. See 'Hut directory', 'Kasseler Hut', 'Day walks' for the route description.

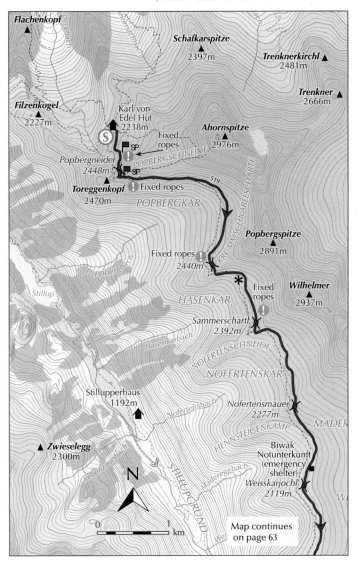

Flachenkopf ▲

Schafkarspitze ▲
2397m

Trenknerkirchl ▲
2481m

Trenkner ▲
2666m

Filzenkogel ▲
2227m

Karl von
Edel Hut
2238m

Ahornspitze ▲
2976m

Popbergneider
2448m

Fixed
ropes

POPBERGSCHNEIDE

Toreggenkopf
2470m

Fixed ropes

POPBERGKAR

519

Popbergspitze ▲
2891m

Fixed ropes
2440m

KRUMMSCHNABELSCHARTE

Fixed
ropes

Wilhelmer ▲
2937m

HASENKAR

Sammerscharth
2392m

NOFERTENSCHNEIDE

NOFERTENSKAR

Stillupperhaus
1192m

Nofertensmauer
2277m

MADER

Zwieselegg ▲
2300m

HENNSTEIGENKAMP

Biwak
Notunterkunft
(emergency
shelter)
Weisskarjoch
2119m

N

0   1
km

Map continues
on page 63

61

At the Popbergneider, en route to the Kasseler Hut

Excellent views and scenery unfold as the route starts to open up.

From the hut, follow Route 519 (signpost) on a good path heading S, climbing gradually first then more steeply across rocky slopes, with fixed ropes at the top, to the little col, visible from the hut, called the **Popbergneider (2448m)**. ¾hr ◄

From the col, descend very steep rocks and grassy slopes, aided by fixed wire ropes, and head E towards the large open combe of the **Popbergkar**. Cross this in a wide arc, first E then S through boulder fields to the foot of a rock face. A short and difficult scramble, aided by fixed ropes, follows to gain the ridge just to the east of the **Krummschnabelscharte col (2440m)**, on the south-west ridge coming down from the Popbergspitze (2891m). 1¾hr

Cross the col, descend steep rocks diagonally across the rock face, aided by fixed ropes, and again head first E then S across difficult open ground of large boulders and blocks across the Hasenkar couloir until stopped by the near-vertical rock wall below the col of the **Sammerschartl (2392m)**. Climb slowly up the 100m of very steep, rocky slabs, aided by gymnasium-style ropes,

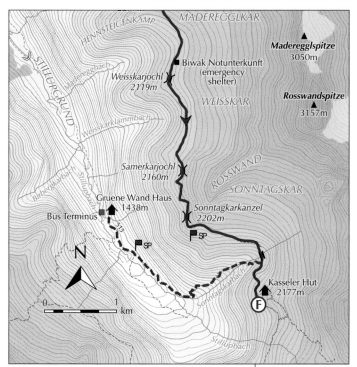

to gain the col and Nofertenschneide ridge on the south-west ridge of the Wilhelmer (2937m). **1¼hr**

From the col, descend steep rocks, aided by fixed ropes, and cross the less-demanding Nofertenkar boulder field to the rock wall of **Nofertensmauer (2277m)** on the Hennsteigenkamp ridge. **1hr**

Exit routes

Should you be forced to consider abandoning the route, you should do so at this point as it is the only place on the route that will allow a descent. Descend W on the north side of the col to pick up forest trails at Nofertenalm, following the exceedingly steep tracks to the alm at

Stillupperhaus. However, it is much safer and easier to return to the sanctuary of the Edel Hut, despite having to reverse the Sammerschartl, where a comfortable bed and good food would make the return journey more acceptable. You should, however, take into consideration that the most difficult sections are behind you, the terrain gets progressively easier and you are a little over halfway into completing the journey.

Main route

Continue S over broken ground, sometimes boulders and then easy paths, to make good time across the Madereggalm, where there are some semi-abandoned farm buildings. One of these huts has been patched up in recent years by the DAV Aschaffenburg Sektion (noted on the maps as **Biwak Notunterkunft**) and now functions as a bivvy, equipped with a few beds and a stove, for those who find themselves exhausted and as an emergency shelter from the weather. It's a good place to take a break. Thereafter, move across the Weisskarjochl (2119m) to the **Samerkarjochl col (2160m)**, on the south-west ridge of the Rosswand. **1¾hr**

Cross the Samerkarl and Steinkarl combes on good paths to reach the last of the ridges to be crossed, the **Sonntagkarkanzel (2202m)**, named as a place for a Sunday church service. ◄ Similarly, you can observe the track across the Lapenscharte, the route to the Greizer Hut, across the great void to the south-west.

From this point you can see the Kasseler Hut, which looks tantalisingly close.

From the col proceed E in a contouring traverse, descending steep grassy slopes interspersed with streams, then head S, losing a couple of hundred metres of height, to a makeshift bridge, usually a single wooden plank over fast-flowing streams, and the junction with the path coming up the valley from Gruene Wand Haus (signpost). Thereafter, follow the zigzag rocky path for a further half hour to the **Kasseler Hut**. **2hr**

EXCURSION

Ascent of Wollbachspitze (3210m) south-west ridge

Start	Kasseler Hut (2177m)
Distance	About 8km
Ascent	1030m
Grade	F+
Standard time	Ascent 4hr; descent 3hr

This is a justifiable and popular day's outing from the Kasseler Hut with a straightforward glacier climb followed by a rock and snow scramble on a much-underrated peak. Sadly, due to the retreat of the Oestliches Stillupkees glacier, the route is now in decline to the extent that only a brief description is provided here. It is advisable to check with the Huettenwirt at the Kasseler hut and consult the hut book for recent ascents before setting out.

The scenic interest, however, remains excellent towards the north-east face of the Grosser Loeffler. The panoramic view from the summit along the Frontier ridge towards the Zillertal's central massif, and more so east towards the Venediger Group of mountains, is particularly good.

CAUTIONARY NOTES

The Wollbachspitze, the first major snow peak you encounter on the ZRR, is a fine climb now spoiled by a difficult approach. Rubble and loose blocks have to be negotiated to access the rapidly retreating Oestliches Stillupkees glacier and Stangenjoch pass, followed by very mixed ground to the summit.

From the hut follow signpost directions for Route 502 to the signpost for the path to the Greizer Hut. **¼hr**

Turn off left, uphill through boulder fields, to a signpost for the panoramic viewpoint of **Schoene Aussicht**. Continue SE to a large stone **cairn** by a glacial pond. **1hr** Continue over difficult ground of boulders and loose

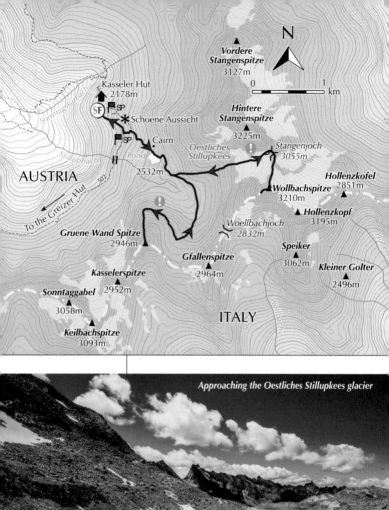

N

Vordere
Stangenspitze
3127m

0   1
|___|___|___|___|___|
                 km

Kasseler Hut
2178m

SF

Schoene Aussicht

Hintere
Stangenspitze
3225m

Cairn

SP

Pond

Oestliches
Stillupkees

Stangenjoch
3055m

AUSTRIA

Stillupbach

502

2532m

Wollbachspitze
3210m

Hollenzkofel
2851m

Hollenzkopf
3195m

To the Greizer Hut

Woellbachjoch
2832m

Speiker
3062m

Gruene Wand Spitze
2946m

Gfallenspitze
2964m

Kleiner Golter
2496m

Kasselerspitze
2952m

ITALY

Wollbach

Sonntaggabel
3058m

Keilbachspitze
3093m

Approaching the Oestliches Stillupkees glacier

blocks, more E, to the foot of the **Oestliches Stillupkees glacier**. **1hr**

Access the glacier at 2900m, heading E to the obvious **Stangenjoch col (3055m)**. While it is almost all dead ice, there are still some crevasses midway. **1hr** From the col head S and scramble over loose boulders, blocks and patches of snow to the summit of **Wollbachspitze (3210m)** with its large wooden cross. **¾hr**

At the summit there are excellent views of the Italian South Tirol and the Grosser Loeffler.

In descent, return by the same route. **3hr**

EXCURSION

Ascent of
Gruene Wand Spitze (2946m)

Start	Kasseler Hut (2177m)
Distance	6km
Ascent	770m
Grade	F+
Standard time	Ascent 3hr; descent 2¼hr
Note	For map, see 'Excursion: Ascent of Wollbachspitze (3210m) south-west ridge'

This excellent promenade takes in stunning scenery on a peak that does not get the attention it deserves.

Apart from the general narrative to point you in the right direction, route finding on this particular climb is rather ad hoc in the middle section until you reach the ridge proper and the climb becomes obvious.

Once on the ridge the mountaineering situation is superb, with lots of good alpine scenery, particularly of the Grosser Loeffler and its close neighbour, the Wollbachspitze. From the summit, the views across the Italian South Tirol of the Ahrntal valley and the peaks of the Dolomites are superb.

CAUTIONARY NOTES

Since this route is not well frequented, route markings are all but non-existent, making route finding particularly haphazard and ad hoc. Apart from the difficulty of route finding, much of the route crosses a challenging, rocky terrain of slabs and blocks that requires quite a bit of care, particularly along the crest of the ridge.

From the hut, follow the route description for climbing the Wollbachspitze as far as the **glacial pond**, large stone cairn and col on the 2532m contour. **1hr**

Continue to head S into the boulder-strewn glacial corrie-type basin, crossing open, difficult ground for around 500 metres. Look for cairns, as the route is not that well marked, before turning more W, heading for the foot of the east spur coming down from the summit. From here to the north-west you will be able to see a small col on the ridge, noted as point 2869m on the AV map. Make a rising diagonal traverse left over difficult, rocky ground of boulders to the col and junction with the mountain's north ridge. **1hr** ◄ From here on, the route is obvious as it scrambles S along the ridge, ascending the crest over blocks and boulders and other dubious rocks to the summit of **Gruene Wand Spitze**. **About 1hr**

Look out for excellent views from here of the Wollbachspitze and Grosser Loeffler.

From the summit descend by reversing the route in its entirety, noting that traversing the summit ridge will take as much time as it did on the ascent until the west flank ridge is met, marked on the AV map as Markierung 2014. If you took a rope with you, use it to short rope, placing slings here and there to ensure safe passage. Thereafter continue to descend over blocks and slabs until easier ground is reached by the alpine pond and stone cairn, then follow the marked route back to the Kasseler Hut. Allow ½**hr** on the summit ridge, **1hr** to the pond and about ¾**hr** back to the hut

STAGE 3
Kasseler Hut to Greizer Hut

Start	Kasseler Hut (2177m)
Finish	Greizer Hut (2226m)
Distance	9.25km
Ascent	750m
Descent	690m
Standard time	6–7hr

After the previous day's outing from the Karl von Edel Hut, many participants would consider this stage with its stunning scenery and interesting challenges to be a rest day of sorts.

This pleasant day's outing presents no major obstacles, the track being well defined throughout, although perhaps made a little awkward in various places by patches of snow, rock-avalanche debris and jumbo-sized boulders.

The scenic interest early in the day is dominated by the view towards the Grosser Loeffler and, later, the view down the valley into Stillupgrund and across the steep slopes of the Siebenschneidenweg, which allows most of the route between the Karl von Edel Hut and the Kasseler Hut to be seen.

Once over the Lapenscharte, new scenery opens up with the Floitenkees and Schwarzensteinkees glaciers and the Grosser Moeseler and Zsigmondyspitze, famed as a rock-climbing peak. But the best scenery of the day is saved for the end when, at the turn of an insignificant zigzag, the Greizer Hut comes splendidly into view with spectacular wall-to-wall mountain scenery.

CAUTIONARY NOTES

This is very much a straightforward walk on well-defined tracks, the main dangers being an area of rock-avalanche debris 1hr after leaving the hut, followed by patches of steep snow and a fixed-rope section crossing the near-vertical, steep-sided Lapen Kar-Elsenklamm buttress. Remember, these ropes are mainly for ski tourers who will cross this area, fully laden with skis and rucksack, when the slopes are still covered with snow.

Summer walkers should find this crossing straightforward; however, those who are not entirely vertigo free should stay close to a companion for moral support and assistance.

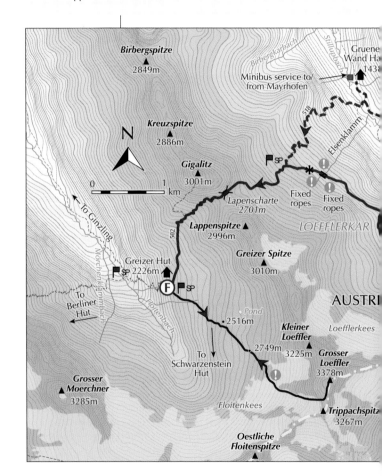

From the hut follow signposts for Route 502, marked as the 'Berliner Hoehenweg', first SE to the junction with the track leading to the Wollbachspitze. ¼hr Continue as before on the main track, turning more SW, where after a further 20min you will come to a door in the middle of nowhere. ▸ Immediately thereafter is a **suspension bridge** for crossing over the raging glacial melt waters

The door is the work of German artist Gunther Rauch and is one of several doors he has erected in the Alps.

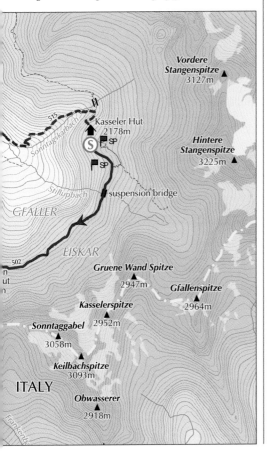

71

coming down from high above. After a short distance further the well-defined track disappears altogether, thanks to a rock avalanche that tore the track apart. Cross this area with care, as the slope is unstable, and then continue as before, traversing the slopes in a wide arc, roughly on the 2300m contour, through the extensive boulder fields of the **Eiskar** to a point approximately north of the Francbach Jochl on the Austrian-Italian border. **1hr** Take in the excellent scenery hereabouts.

The route now turns more or less N to traverse the steep slopes of the **Loefflerkar**. ◄ Fixed ropes are provided to aid stability when negotiating the near-vertical buttress and difficult sections that form the Elsenklamm gorge. **3hr** Look back towards the Wollbachspitze for excellent views.

Continue NW through the Lapenkar boulder field to join up with Route 518 (signpost) on the 2800m contour, which marks the route coming up from Gruene Wand Haus at the top end of the Stillupgrund valley, located to the north-east. **¾hr**

The route turns SW and continues to climb steeply in a series of long, looping zigzags, negotiating difficult

This midsection is frequently dotted with patches of snow and melt water streaming down from the upper slopes of the Loefflerkees glacier.

At the suspension bridge, with Grosser Loeffler in the distance

ground through boulders of car-sized proportions and crossing patches of snow to the **Lapenscharte (2701m)**, formed in a tight gap between the peaks of Gigalitz (3001m) and the tad higher Greizer Spitze (3010m). **1hr**

At the col there are excellent vistas, particularly across the void towards the Rosswandspitze in the east, and there is an opportunity to review the long walk from the Karl von Edel Hut – especially for those who made the effort to cross the Siebenschneidenweg. Looking in the opposite direction, you can recce the route to the Berliner Hut across the Moerchenscharte and the ladder section at the foot of the ridge.

From the col, descend steeply SW over rough, broken ground through more boulder fields, which have become a characteristic of this walk. At the 2400m contour, about 20min from the Lapenscharte, the route turns S into the Griesfeld from where, after a short distance, the wonderfully sited Greizer Hut, complete with attendant peaks, gleaming glaciers and even the Schwarzenstein Hut at the head of the Floitenkees glacier, comes into superb view. The route, now obvious, continues along a fine paved rock gallery to the **Greizer Hut**. **1½hr**

EXCURSION
Ascent of Grosser Loeffler (3379m)

Start	Greizer Hut (2226m)
Distance	8km
Ascent	1155m
Grade	PD+
Standard time	Ascent 5hr; descent 4hr
Note	For map, see Stage 3

First climbed by Martin Lipolt and party in 1850, the Grosser Loeffler is one of the best and most interesting mountains in the Zillertal. The route is mostly a glacier tour with a route-finding exercise on the Floitenkees glacier, which deservedly gives the route the title of the most crevassed climb in the Zillertal!

Sadly, due to the retreat of the Floitenkees glacier in recent years, the route is in decline to such an extent that only a brief description is provided here. It is advisable to check with the Huettenwirt at the Greizer Hut and consult the hut book for recent ascents before setting out.

The scenic interest is excellent, with the glacial scenery being superb. One cannot help wondering how much longer such an expanse of ice can last as the environment adjusts to global warming.

CAUTIONARY NOTES

While the route carries an alpine grade of F+ in other guides, this is woefully inadequate due to the complexity of the climb through the Floitenkees glacier and the very serious crevasse dangers. The route should be regraded PD+ to take into account the sustained difficulties, since there is nothing easy about this route.

While the route to the glacier is straightforward, you are advised to do a route-finding recce before leaving the hut, as the trail is not well marked. Thereafter, once on the glacier, good judgement is necessary to navigate a route through the crevasses – some of which are in complex groups, and all of which will have to be reversed in descent.

Obviously, this route should not be undertaken in less than fair weather when route finding would be made difficult and dangerous in the extreme.

From the hut (signpost) head SE over rocks through the **Griesfeld boulder field** to point 2516m on the AV map. **1hr**

Continue SE over difficult ground, with rocks of car-sized proportions, to a point below the Kleiner Loeffler at 2749m, where it should be possible to get onto the right (N) bank of the **Floitenkees glacier**. **1hr**

Once on the glacier, head S first to round a buttress and blind ridge, then turn SW up the glacier, negotiating several crevasse zones, some of which are quite complex. Once past the foot of the Grosser Loeffler's west ridge, proceed E up the steep, glaciated, crevassed

The route as seen from the Trippachsattel

slope, heading for point 3292m on the ridge between the Grosser Loeffler and the Trippachspitze. **1hr**

Remember while ascending that you will also have to return by the same route. Using the old pioneering trick, you can leave some route markers to aid your descent, such as a pile of stones, a glove, a scarf, basically anything that will aid your descent until you reach safe ground.

Cross the bergschrund, then traverse N to gain the upper slopes of the west ridge where it abuts the main south ridge. **1hr**

It is hereabouts that a light **aircraft** crashed in 1996, sadly killing its occupants. While there may still be odd bits of the aircraft on the mountain, most of the wreckage has been removed by the Austrian military.

Get onto the rocks and climb the very difficult, steep, mixed ground over rocks and snow to gain the south ridge proper and continue a short distance to the summit of **Grosser Loeffler** with its large metal cross – excellent mountaineering! **1hr**

The panoramic **views** from the summit are extensive: to the north are the mountains of the Karwendel on the Austro-German border; to the south the Italian Dolomites; to the east the mountains of the Venediger and Grossglockner; while close by, across the glacial expanse of the Schwarzenstein, is the Zillertal's highest peak, the Hochfeiler, and beyond, the Oetztal and Stubai Alps.

In descent, reverse the route in its entirety, taking care on the ridge's rocky sections, placing running belays when moving together. Similarly, once on the Floitenkees glacier, maintain good glacier travel techniques through the maze of crevasses until you reach safe ground on the Griesfeld boulder slopes. **Allow 4hr**

STAGE 4
Greizer Hut to Berliner Hut

Start	Greizer Hut (2226m)
Finish	Berliner Hut (2042m)
Distance	9km
Ascent	1050m
Decent	1230m
Standard time	6–8hr

There are two options to choose from when deciding your route from the Greizer Hut to the Berliner Hut. The first route is the official route of the Zillertal Rucksack Route, while the second is a variant and demanding alpine tour that takes in the Floitenkees glacier and Schwarzenstein Hut prior to descending to the Berliner Hut.

It is not often on the ZRR that you start the day walking downhill, but this is how this walk begins and sadly well over 400m is lost in the initial stages, which is regained on the steep, muscle-tugging climb to the Moerchenscharte. But first there is a ladder section to negotiate, which some will find intimidating while others will find it fun.

The early part of the day lacks any real views due to the loss of height, but good views re-establish themselves when you reach the little saddle at 2287m, with excellent scenery towards the Floitenkees glacier and around to the Grosser Loeffler and the Schwarzenstein group. Time should be taken here for a second breakfast stop, as there are no other suitable stopping places until you reach the Moerchenscharte.

Thereafter, the Moerchenscharte provides a good mountaineering-type situation. And once you reach the col at the top, and the end of the day's difficulties, the route opens up with a particularly splendid view across the void to the snowy mantel of Grosser Moeseler.

The photo opportunities on the walk down from the Moerchenscharte are excellent and none more so than at Schwarzsee lake and then just above the Berliner Hut, when the hut, pride of the German Alpine Club, and Grosser Moeseler are in view.

CAUTIONARY NOTES

To reach the walk proper, you will need to negotiate streams and a ladder. Thereafter, take care on the top section of the approach to the Moerchenscharte, as the ground is very steep and quite loose in places. Make good use of the fixed wires and your improvised harness to ensure you stay safe. Participants should also note that late winter snow on the west side of the Moerchenscharte can be quite problematic if there is a lot of it.

In the event of bad weather, you would be better advised to stay put in the comfortable Greizer Hut or take 4hr and descend to Ginzling, then get the Postbus to Breitlahner, followed by the 3hr walk to the Berliner Hut to continue the tour. However, this detour is not easy to accomplish in one day, and it may be wiser to overnight in Breitlahner or Ginzling before continuing.

Allow extra time if you have youngsters with you, and be on your way by 07:00.

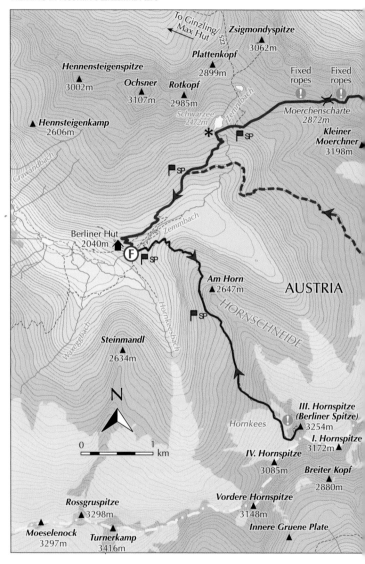

To Ginzling/Max Hut

Zsigmondyspitze
3062m

Plattenkopf
2899m

Hennensteigenspitze
3002m

Ochsner
3107m

Rotkopf
2985m

Fixed ropes   Fixed ropes

Moerchenscharte
2872m

Kleiner Moerchner
3198m

Hennsteigenkamp
2606m

Schwarzee
2472m

*

Berliner Hut
2040m

Am Horn
2647m

AUSTRIA

HORNSCHNEIDE

Steinmandl
2634m

N

0   1   km

Hornkees

III. Hornspitze
(Berliner Spitze)
3254m

I. Hornspitze
3172m

IV. Hornspitze
3085m

Breiter Kopf
2880m

Vordere Hornspitze
3148m

Innere Gruene Plate

Rossgruspitze
3298m

Moeselenock
3297m

Turnerkamp
3416m

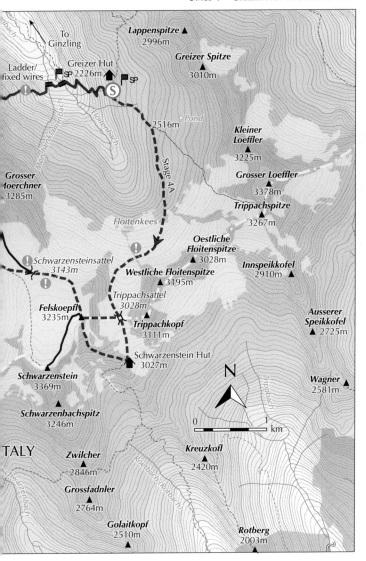

Moerchenscharte

The route to the Moerchenscharte, as seen from the Greizer Hut

From the hut, descend W, following signposts for Route 502 for the Berliner Hoehenweg and Berliner Hut, generally heading in the direction of the lovely village of Ginzling to a point at 1800m where the route divides (signpost for Berliner Hut and Ginzling). **1hr**

Cross open ground to the west through boulders and across glacial streams, some more torrent than babbling brook, negotiating old snow and avalanche debris, to a footbridge to cross the raging torrents coming down from the Floitenkees glacier. **1hr**

Continue W for a short distance to the foot of the Moerchenklamm gorge and the obvious adjacent buttress and ridge coming down from the Moerchenscharte. The track continues over rough ground, where route finding is not always obvious due to annual avalanche debris; look for cairns and the usual daubs of red paint route markers. The route, as such, then rises steeply, at which point you will be confronted with a 6m-high **ladder**, followed by a series of **fixed ropes**, to get round the buttress onto easier ground.

This section is not hard but it is exposed to some sizeable drops; those who are not entirely vertigo free should stay close to a companion, and everyone should make use of an improvised harness as this is no place to risk a fall.

The route now follows a track to and fro up the edge of the ridge to a small saddle noted as point 2287m on the AV map. This provides a much-needed breathing space and is a good place to stop for a quick snack. From this point you can try to work out the original route to and from the Greizer Hut, which made a contouring traverse across and around the then lower section of the Floitenkees glacier. Sadly, the route no longer exists, no doubt blown away by avalanche, but it may be undertaken in winter by experienced ski mountaineers, but for us walkers we can only wonder.

Thereafter, at our modest level, the route continues steeply upward through a narrow couloir, often with patches of snow on loose, rocky ground, aided in places by fixed wires, to exit at the obvious col that is the **Moerchenscharte (2872m)** on the south ridge of the Grosser Moerchner (3285m). **3–4hr**

> While at the Moerchenscharte, take time to review the panoramic **view** back towards the Greizer Hut, which is now isolated in an expanse of mountains that form the Frontier ridge with Italy, running in a wide arc from the Grosser Loeffler and around the great expanse of ice that forms the Floitenkees and Schwarzensteinkees glaciers. In the opposite direction, towards the south-west, is the route to the Furtschaglhaus across the Schoenbichlerscharte (3081m), the highest pass on the ZRR and the only pass over the magic height of 3000m.

From the col the descent route is obvious, with the Berliner Hut being just over 2hr away. Continue W, descending a steep track, frequently snow covered in early season and with fixed wires in place on the steep sections, through an area known as the Rosskar. ▶ After a short distance the scenery starts to open up to include the pointed peak of the Berliner Spitze and its attendant

Many tiny vivid purple and orange toadflax flowers grow in this area.

At Schwarzsee

Hornkees ridge. Eventually, you will see the intersection of paths, with Route 522 heading N to the Max Hut, via the Eissee and Melkerscharte, to the charming village of Ginzling. Sharp eyes will also be able to locate the very substantial Berliner Hut far below (signpost).

Continue the downwards journey, where, after a few more minutes, the track overlooks the tiny picturesque alpine lake that is the **Schwarzsee** at 2472m. **1hr**

> Once at the tiny lake, if the weather is good, take time and make a 5min detour to the north shoreline, which will provide an excellent foreground to frame picture-postcard views of the Berliner Spitze and Hornspitze group of mountains reflected on the little sea's surface. This is five-star mountain scenery at its best.

Continue as before, first past an abandoned shepherd's hut, then following the well-defined path, many parts of which have been painstakingly paved with large stone pavers, to the junction of routes leading to and from the Schwarzensteinkees glacier, used by aspiring alpinists participating in the Sud Tirol Tour (signpost).

With the Berliner Hut now more clearly in sight, it is a simple matter of following the well-worn trail of Route 502 to its natural conclusion at the hut. **1hr**

But before making those last few steps, take a moment to recce the route to the Furtschaglhaus over the Schoenbichlerscharte, which can be viewed in its entirety from the picturesque path to the very grand **Berliner Hut**.

Alternative poor weather route option
Should you be unfortunate to have bad weather while at the Greizer Hut and wish to continue with the tour, the following is a reluctant action plan.

In the event of bad weather, it is wise to book the Floitental shuttle. But remember, if the weather is foul, you will not be the only ones looking to reserve the shuttle service. As the advertisement says, 'Book early to avoid disappointment!' Floitental shuttle taxi service tel 0043 664 102 9354.

From the hut descend and follow the route description as far as the signpost pointing the way to the Moerchenscharte and Berliner Hut. From here continue to descend the track until it widens into the forest service road and terminates at the *Seilbahn*, the material goods hoist for the hut. If you have played your cards right, you will have pre-booked the Floitental shuttle taxi service, which will whisk you down the valley to Ginzling, or better still deposit you at the Bergbauernhof Hotel at Breitlahner. Thereafter, make the 3hr journey to the Berliner Hut. The total journey time is about 6hr. Should you opt to walk all the way to Ginzling, this will take a minimum of 3hr, plus time spent waiting for the bus, plus time taken walking to the Berliner Hut, making a very long day of around 8–9hr.

STAGE 4A
Greizer Hut to Berliner Hut via Floitenkees glacier or Schwarzenstein Hut

Start	Greizer Hut (2226m)
Finish	Berliner Hut (2042m)
Distance	12.75km
Ascent	1100m
Descent	Negligible to the Schwarzenstein Hut; 1150m to the Berliner Hut
Standard time	To the Schwarzenstein Hut 5–6hr; to the Berliner Hut via the Felskoepfl and Schwarzenstein Sattel 8–10hr
Note	For map, see Stage 4

This deviation will add an extra day onto the ZRR's basic itinerary, but if you and your companions are aspiring alpinists and looking to add that little extra spice to your *Bergtour* (mountain hike) – and the weather is good – then this glacial journey comes highly recommended. Of course, fit, strong parties can cut out the middleman and head directly to the Berliner Hut in about 8 to 10 hours if conditions are good. If not, just enjoy the ambience of the futuristic Schwarzenstein Hut's airy perch.

This first-class glacier journey is full of challenge and tremendous alpine scenery throughout. Those who climbed the Grosser Loeffler will have the pleasure of seeing the mountain face on, with its labyrinth of crevasses seen to best advantage.

CAUTIONARY NOTES

This journey is more an exercise in route finding than a test of your ability to climb, so it should only be undertaken in good weather and is to be avoided after a fresh snowfall due to crevasse dangers. The route is not to be underestimated, as it is a serious glacier journey comparable with any in the Alps.

Sadly, due to the retreat of the Floitenkees glacier in recent years, the route is now in decline to the extent that the description provided here is indicative and will change. Would-be participants should seek the advice of the *Huettenwirt* at the Greizer Hut, and consult the entries in the hut book, to see if the route is possible before setting out.

Participants should also remember that once they have crossed into Italy they are committed to the route as there is no easy way back into Austria. Should the weather turn bad, you may be forced to have a prolonged stay in the South Tirol or, alternatively, descend into Italy and make a long return journey to Austria via Sterzing and the Brenner pass.

Greizer Hut to the Schwarzenstein Hut

From the hut, follow the same obvious track as for the Grosser Loeffler, heading SE towards the Floitenkees glacier. The track rises steeply in a series of steps over rocks and boulders, passing a small pond where after about an hour you will come to a large boulder with 'Trippachsattel' written on it. **1hr** Bear off right, heading towards the glacier. Proceed carefully here over difficult ground, through boulders and other glacial rubble, to reach the **Floitenkees glacier** at around 2600m. ▶ Look for makeshift stone cairns as the route varies from year to year. Gear up and ensure your Prusik loops are in place and all other tackle is accessible should you need it. **1hr**

Note this area is likely to change as the glacier recedes and access becomes more problematic.

Which way? New snow makes it more difficult to cross the Floitenkees glacier

Get onto the glacier, setting a course to cross the ice in a wide arc. First, head S, climbing steeply to a point below the Oestliche Floitenspitze. Then make an oblique traverse left to right, passing the foot of the **Westliche Floitenspitze**. ◄ Cross the heavily crevassed glacial basin, taking extra care hereabouts, heading W for the obvious rock buttress coming down from the **Felskoepfl** on the 3000m contour. **2hr**

Do not linger here as the route is subject to stonefall.

To continue to the Schwarzenstein Hut from the 3000m contour, head S and take a direct path to the obvious snowy plateau that is the **Trippachsattel** at 3028m on the Austrian-Italian ridge; look out for a very large sign-post that marks the border.

From the col/saddle, the copper-clad **Schwarzenstein Hut** is clearly visible on the rocky rib of the Trippachschneide ridge, some 650 metres away. See 'Hut directory' for details of the Schwarzenstein Hut.

Continue across the right bank of the Trippachkees glacier and simply scramble over rocks to the superbly sited **Schwarzenstein Hut**. **1hr**

Schwarzenstein Hut to the Berliner Hut

To continue to the Berliner Hut, initially retrace your steps and climb the rocks at the back of the hut followed by a steepish snowfield that leads to the summit of the **Felskoepfl** (3235m) at the southern tip of the Schwarzenstein's east ridge. **1hr+** Head NW across the glacier. From here, you can continue to the **Schwarzensteinsattel**, allowing around 3½hr to the Berliner Hut, or alternatively, and highly recommended, suitably inspired participants may wish to make a 1hr detour and bag the Schwarzenstein (3369m) by traversing the mountain via the Frontier ridge before descending to the **Berliner Hut**.

There are excellent views across the entire Zillertal, the South Tirol, the Rieserferner Group and beyond to the Dolomites.

Descend NW on the rounded snow rib, bypassing crevasses, to point 3143m on the **Schwarzensteinsattel**, midway across the glacier, at the foot of the Grosser Moerchner's south ridge. ▸

From the saddle, descend the Schwarzensteinkees glacier in a westerly direction – beware of crevasses midway – heading for a *rognon* (rocky island) at 2945m. Leave the glacier and scramble down rocks – some have fixed wires and one gully is fitted with a short ladder – then across patches of snow to reach easy ground. **2hr** The route is waymarked from here on, descending a rocky trail through the Moerchnerkar boulder field to eventually meet up with the standard route (Stage 4) over the **Moerchenscharte** at point 2256m (signpost). **1hr** (plus a further **1hr** to reach the Berliner Hut)

Shortcut between Trippachsattel and Felskoepfl, avoiding Schwarzenstein Hut

From the 3000m contour just below the **Trippachsattel**, head W through the upper snowfields and rocky outcrops, climbing steadily through the rocks to point 3140m, from where the upper reaches of the glacier flatten out below the **Felskoepfl**. In good conditions, strong parties may climb the very steep upper snow slope directly, keeping right (N), avoiding the traverse through the rocks. **2hr**

The route now joins up with the route from the Schwarzenstein Hut.

From here a 1hr round-trip detour can be made to the summit of the Moerchner before you vacate the gleaming glacier slopes for the Berliner Hut.

EXCURSION

Ascent of the Berliner Spitze
(Hornspitze III) (3254m)

Start	Berliner Hut (2042m)
Distance	8km
Ascent	1215m
Grade	PD-
Standard time	Ascent 4–5hr; descent 3–4hr
Note	For map, see Stage 4

This excellent climb over mixed ground on a popular peak provides that much-needed experience for aspiring alpinists to differentiate between routes graded *Facile* (easy), *Peu Difficile* (a little difficult) or *Assez Difficile* (moderately difficult). This route is graded PD-, mostly because of the mixed climbing involved.

The approach to the climb is excellent, with scenic interest provided by the dominant wedge of Turnerkamp's north face, a mountain with no easy route to the top.

Once you step off the glacier and onto the ridge, the feeling of open space is superb, with fine alpine scenery in all directions, particularly towards the glacial expanse of the Schwarzenstein glacier. This continues to improve and is only bettered once on the summit; here there is an opportunity to see over the other side of the mountain deep into Italy and the South Tirol, with the jagged peaks of the Dolomites breaking the skyline on the southern horizon, then, more closely along the Frontier ridge, Turnerkamp and the lofty summits of the Grosser Moeseler and Hochfeiler.

CAUTIONARY NOTES

As the Hornkees glacier is now in decline, it mainly comprises dead ice covered with snow and presents minimal crevasse danger. However, the snow slope remains steep and, for most sensible parties, still warrants roping up. Most of the objective dangers on this climb are quite obvious and require nothing more than basic rock and ice mountaineering skills to overcome them.

In descent, care should be exercised in climbing down the steeper sections; these should be reversed and down climbed in a series of short pitches to place running belays to get onto the glacier.

While route finding is not normally a problem, like most mountains in the region, hot, moist air coming from the south soon starts to build cloud by mid morning, making the descent from the summit and across the glacier more problematic if you are late in the day.

From the hut proceed E, following the path below the hut to get across the **Zemmbach river** (signpost for the Berliner Spitze). **¼hr**

The track continues E, heading for the obvious long north-west ridge coming down from the Hornspitze.

Climb the rock buttress in a series of long looping zigzags through dwarf alpine rose and juniper bushes, over slabs and rocky ground, until the route turns SE below the **Am Horn** to follow the general line of the Hornschneide ridge (signpost). **1hr**

Proceed over rocks and boulders along the Horn Weg in a rising traverse, sometimes on paved slabs that have been painstakingly laid out. In total contrast at the midpoint, the track heads through a series of rockfalls, with boulders of car-sized proportions, and similar ankle-twisting terrain which eventually peters out when the track meets the **Hornkees glacier** on the 2900m contour. **1hr**

Tackle up, get onto the Hornkees glacier and continue SE on the north edge of the right bank, heading for a rock island immediately below an obvious col on the ridge above.

Continue as before up the steepening snow slope, heading for the obvious col of the Mittelbachjoch and its excellent mountaineering-type scenery. **1hr** Exit the glacier and climb through the rocks, patches of snow and short sections of Grade II scrambling; take care and use

Climbing the Berliner Spitze

Berliner Spitze

Mittelbachjoch

Hornkees glacier

To/from Berliner Hut

in-situ belays when moving together, as the rock is loose in places, to emerge on the summit of the **Berliner Spitze (3254m)**, with its large wooden cross. Superb alpine scenery extends towards the peaks of the Schwarzenstein and the majestic Turnerkamp. **1hr**

From the summit return by the same route, exiting the glacier at the starting point on the rocky moraine at 2900m.

From this point, reverse the journey back to the Berliner Hut – but be warned: do not attempt to make a shortcut and detour below the Am Horn back to the hut, as there are several steep rock faces to negotiate, remnants left long ago by the retreating Hornkees glacier. **Allow 3–4hr**

STAGE 5
Berliner Hut to Furtschaglhaus

Start	Berliner Hut (2042m)
Finish	Furtschaglhaus (2295m)
Distance	8km
Ascent	1020m
Descent	850m
Standard time	6–7hr

This fine excursion, while not unduly difficult, marks the ascent of the highest pass on the ZRR, being the only one to cross the magical 3000m contour without having to climb a mountain.

The route has excellent scenic interest throughout, particularly around the 2500m contour, where the panoramic backdrop to the Berliner Hut and Moerchenscharte is particularly fine. Thereafter, the scene is dominated in ascent by the Grosser Moeseler, then in descent by the Zillertal's highest peak, the Hochfeiler. From the top of the Schoenbichler Horn, there is a stunning view of wall-to-wall mountains.

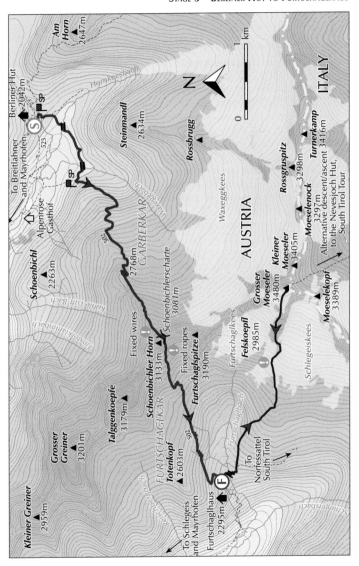

CAUTIONARY NOTES

This is quite a long day with over 1000m of uphill to negotiate and a high pass to cross, which means you need to be on your way early, preferably no later than 07:00.

Apart from crossing the footbridge over the Waxeggbach river early in the day (not to be underestimated), the main difficulties lie in negotiating the steep sections on both sides of the Schoenbichlerscharte, the upper sections of which usually retain a fair amount of old hard-packed snow late into the season. Both sides of the pass have fixed ropes to aid stability; the ground is very steep and not that good underfoot. Using the ropes is essential when carrying a big rucksack and do make use of your long sling and karabiner as your improvised, rudimentary harness.

Avoid this route in poor weather, when route finding becomes increasingly problematic. In heavy rain the Schoenbichlerscharte runs with water, and it is not a place to be caught in a thunderstorm, when the fixed wires zing with electricity.

In bad weather participants on a tight schedule are advised to cut their losses and descend to Breitlahner to get the bus to Schlegeis, omitting the Furtschaglhaus, and then take the short alternative walk to the congenial Olperer Hut.

As you leave the pride of the German Alpine Club behind, a signpost on the hut's terrace points the way to the Furtschaglhaus with now familiar signs for Route 502 and the 'Berliner-Zillertal Hoehenweg', also known as the Central Alpine Way.

Follow the track down the rocky slope for a few metres to a substantial bridge just below the hut to get across the raging torrents of the Zemmbach river (signpost).

Continue as directed, following the track for a further 10min to a vague junction of paths with a **signpost** pointing the way to the right and the Schoenbichler Horn, ignoring the track directly ahead that leads to an obvious cabin. ◄

From here there are good views of the Berliner Spitze.

Continue to descend on a gravel path for a short distance to a double-plank-type **footbridge** across the **Hornkeesbach** stream, with adjacent signpost.

Continue as before, traversing a rocky terrain of glacier-scoured granite slabs and boulder fields, aided in parts by steel pegs and ladder staples, to round the slope leading to the first real challenge of the day: crossing a second unguarded plank **footbridge** over the very noisy **Waxeggbach** river. **1hr**

Be careful here as the approach to the bridge is over precarious, water-scoured boulders, which can be an intimidating experience for children and for those who are not entirely sure-footed. Make good use of trekking poles to aid balance, and avoid crossing the river if it's in spate and the approach to the bridge is flooded. If in doubt, return to the Berliner Hut and take the alternative, much-safer route via the Alpenrose Hut.

Cross the footbridge and follow the obvious track. From here, the route begins to ramp up, and after a few minutes you will reach the glacial moraine ridge and an old **signpost** pointing the way to Furtschaglhaus. The route now makes a left turn (S) and starts to climb the obvious rocky rib of the moraine. After another short distance you will reach a myriad of signs along with the junction of the path rising from the Alpenrose Hut, which can be seen far below. ▸

From here on, simply climb the rocky ridge, following the line of the moraine until it finally relents and turns right (NW), following long looping zigzags to enter the upper combe leading to the Garberkar boulder field. **Approx 1½hr**

The track then pitches up as the ground starts to rise more steeply to follow glacial debris through an open couloir that forms the **Garberkar**. Follow the rocky slopes to 2600m and the junction with the old track that heads S onto the Waxeggkees glacier. Excellent views open up of the Waxeggkees glacier and the north flank of the Grosser Moeseler to the Moeselerscharte.

Continue SW, hugging the ridge, with the track rising in a series of steep zigzags over wearisome, difficult ground first through boulders then rock, shale, scree and patches of snow. The path of sorts rises more steeply at the top, where for the last 100m you are aided by fixed

From here there are excellent views down the Zemmgrund valley and back across the void to the Berliner Hut and the Moerchenscharte.

Negotiating difficult, steep ground aided by fixed ropes at the Schoenbichlerscharte, an area frequently covered with hard snow

wire ropes to emerge on the rocky **Schoenbichlerscharte** at 3081m. Here you will be greeted with great views of the Hochfeiler's north face and beyond and a whole new vista of mountain scenery to enjoy. **2–2½hr**

To ascend the Schoenbichler Horn
From the col, which is only large enough to allow a few folk to mingle, it is possible to make the 5min excursion and scramble up the final steep, rocky slopes to the

Hochfeiler (3510m; far right), the highest peak in the Zillertal

summit of the **Schoenbichler Horn** (3133m). At the top you will obtain even better views of the adjacent Grosser Moeseler and the glacial expanse of the Hochfeiler, as well as views across the void to the Olperer and retrospectively to the Moerchnerscharte, giving you an opportunity to review the whole journey so far.

In descent, the upper section of the Schoenbichlerscharte is frequently covered with hard snow for the first 50m or so. Take care!

Main route
From the col descend difficult, steep ground through an open rocky gulley, zigzagging to and fro to get round the steep rocks, patches of snow, loose rocks and shale – fixed wires are in place on the steeper sections – until the ground gradually eases on the 2700m contour.

With the hut in view, continue SW, now on easier ground, down the ridge of an old glacial moraine, zigzagging through the Furtschaglkar boulder field while enjoying excellent views of the Grosser Moeseler and north face of the Hochfeiler, and onto the **Furtschaglhaus**. **Approx 2hr**

EXCURSION

Ascent of Grosser Moeseler
(3480m) via the west spur

Start	Furtschaglhaus (2295m)
Distance	6km
Ascent	1185m
Grade	PD
Standard time	Ascent 4–5hr; descent to the Furtschaglhaus 3hr; descent to the Edelraut Hut 3–4hr
Note	For map, see Stage 5

Perhaps the most challenging of the mountains on the ZRR, the Grosser Moeseler, the Zillertal's second highest and possibly most scenic of mountains, is a magnificent day out.

The mountain was first climbed from the south (Sud Tirol) by a British party of Fox, Freshfield and Tuckett (Alpine Club), with French guides François Devouassoud and Peter Michel, on a rare visit to the Eastern Alps on 16 June 1865. They reached Zamseralm at 19:00, almost coming to grief several times in the dark.

This is an excellent route in every respect of mountaineering and is one to savour and relish. The summit is a true summit, being steep on all sides and invoking that feeling that you have climbed to the top of something very special. The panoramic view from the summit is extensive in all directions, particularly along the Frontier ridge towards Turnerkamp and the Schwarzenstein, where some crevasses of gigantic proportions may be seen. In the opposite direction, across the great swathe of glacier, lies the classic north face of the Hochfeiler with its close neighbour, Hoher Weisszint. It is all truly splendid indeed.

CAUTIONARY NOTES

The crux of the route is in negotiating the steep, rocky rib of the Felskoepfl, which comprises slabs of rock and flakes standing on edge. It is very steep, with the odd place close to vertical; fortunately, these sections are short, being only 4–6 metres in length, and there is plenty of opportunity to belay and climb safely.

Unless absolutely necessary, the stone couloir should be avoided due to the risk of falling stones, particularly later in the day when parties are coming off the mountain and folk are more likely to dislodge rocks.

From the hut follow signs for the mountain, proceeding first downhill to cross the **Furtschaglbach river**, then commence uphill for 20min, following signposts for the Norfessattel pass on the Italian border and our objective, the Grosser Moeseler.

The route now turns SE, climbing steadily up a ridge of a glacial moraine with some large stone cairns to the 2727m point and, a little further, the junction with the **Schlegeiskees glacier**. **1hr** Tackle up and get onto the glacier, heading E to the foot of an obvious buttress. Cross the glacier, keeping below the ice fall and avoiding several lines of crevasses en route.

Round the buttress until an obvious gully and tight couloir comes into view. Head towards this, climbing steepish snow slopes. Negotiate the bergschrund and get onto the rocky rib on the right-hand side. **1–1¼hr** ▸

Take in the excellent scenery.

Some parties do climb the adjacent couloir directly but note that this acts as a stone chute of sorts and is not entirely safe. More recently, parties have started to climb the buttress to the far left of the couloir, but this is also quite loose at the top.

Climb the rocks to the right-hand side of the couloirs, which steepen considerably at the top with short pitches of moderate to difficult climbing, to exit on the summit snowfield. **1hr** There are some stone marker cairns, but these are not consistent. The summit is obvious from here on, its large wooden cross in clear sight. Climb and cross the snowfield, which is steep in places, heading for a notch to the left of the summit followed by a short, exposed corniced ridge to the summit of **Grosser Moeseler**. **1–1¼hr** There are excellent views in all directions.

On the summit snowfield, with the Olperer top left, Gefrornene-Wand-Spitzen centre and Hoher Riffler centre right

In descent, reverse the route in its entirety. Take time to look over the north-west face, which has extreme, breathtaking vertical exposure together with some tremendous ice cliffs, hanging glaciers and gigantic crevasses. Exercise care and take your time while descending the rocky rib, remembering to place running belays on the steeper sections. Similarly, care is needed when reversing the bergschrund. Thereafter, the rest of the journey should be a pleasant stroll back to the **Furtschaglhaus**. About 3hr

Alternative descent

For those aspiring alpinists who have ambitions to climb the Hochfeiler, climbing the Grosser Moeseler and descending from the summit to the Edelraut Hut or the Nevesjoch Hut in the South Tirol will provide that opportunity.

Apart from the initial stages, the descent route to Edelraut Hut is more straightforward than the ascent from Furtschaglhaus, the route being entirely on rock apart from some patches of snow. **Allow 3–4hr** ◄

See notes for the Zillertal South Tirol Tour Stage 5 and route description under Excursions from the Nevesjoch Hut: 'Ascent of Grosser Moeseler (3480m)'.

STAGE 6
Furtschaglhaus to Olperer Hut

Start	Furtschaglhaus (2295m)
Finish	Olperer Hut (2389m)
Distance	9.25km
Ascent	600m
Descent	500m
Standard time	5–6hr

This is quite an easy day's tour compared with the previous day's outings, and the second stage on the clockwise tour of the ZRR to start off downhill. However, despite this relative ease, it's still a long way to the Olperer Hut, and most groups will take five hours to complete the journey.

Unfortunately, as you leave the Furtschaglhaus, the views of the Grosser Moeseler and Hochfeiler are soon lost. However, a splendid vista of the Olperer, the third-highest peak in the Zillertal, soon comes into view, occupying most of your attention and interest up to the rest area at Zamsgatterl–Jausenstat.

Some would say the walk lapses into something of a plod; plod or not, the walk along the edge of the Schlegeisspeicher reservoir with its forest fringe is a pleasant change from the previous day's exertion on the high peak. Participants who have ambitions of climbing the Olperer should take good note as the route can clearly be seen from the edge of the lake, particularly the Schneegupf snow arête. Similarly, the route from the Olperer Hut to Friesenberghaus is well defined since both huts are clearly visible to the eagle-eyed.

However, the real reward of the day is on reaching the splendid Olperer Hut with its delightful terrace and extensive panoramic view across the Schlegeisspeicher to the Grosser Moeseler and Hochfeiler.

From the hut pick up the trail once more of the ZRR which starts by descending steeply, following the Central Alpine Way, **Route 502**. More steep zigzags lead to an easy path heading NE to the tip of the man-made lake that is the **Schlegeisspeicher hydroelectric reservoir**.

The route then follows a single-track graded service road with good views towards the Olperer and

At Schlegeisspeicher reservoir with the Olperer on the left, the Gefrorene-Wand-Spitzen in the centre and the Hoher Riffler on the right

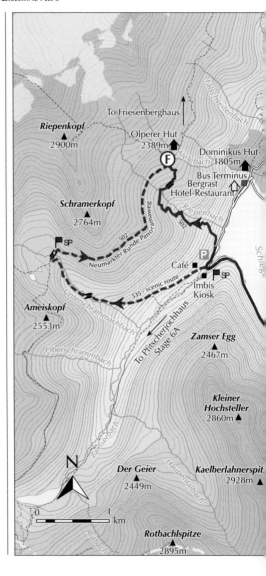

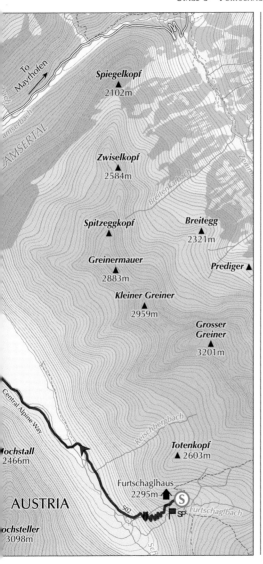

Hoher Riffler, traversing along the base of the Kleiner Hochsteller, adjacent to the lake's left bank, for 3.5km to a large **car park** at Zamsgatterl–Jausenstat, complete with rest area, cafeterias, restaurant and all the trappings of tourism. **2hr**

Despite the commercialism – and my quip – it is a relatively pleasant place to stop and take an extended breather and maybe get something to eat before escaping to loftier places.

Optional detours
Participants with time on their hands can make a one-day detour from the car park and head for the Italian border to stay at the Pfitscherjochhaus (2275m), at the head of the Zamsergrund valley. Then follow Route 528 (see the Peter Habeler Runde Tour Stage 3) towards the Geraer Hut and Alpeiner Scharte before turning off to meet the route to the Olperer Hut. See notes at the end of this section.

Similarly for aspiring alpinists, this is a good place to peel away from the main Zillertal valley and head for the South Tirol, extending the tour by five days for some top-notch hut-to-hut tours and brilliant peaks. See notes for the Zillertal South Tirol Tour.

Main route
Meanwhile at Zamsgatterl–Jausenstat you have a choice of routes to the Olperer Hut.

For the usual and shortest route to the Olperer Hut, continue N along the road in the direction of Mayrhofen, overlooking the reservoir to the Schlegeis restaurant, where a little further on you will find a signpost indicating the way uphill to the Dominikus and Olperer Huts.

> While you wander along the shores of the **Schlegeisspeicher** with its 130m-high dam wall, it is worth pondering the fate of the various buildings and alms that were flooded to make way for progress and the provision of hydroelectricity. One such place was the original Dominikus Hut, which was constructed as a private venture by members of the

OeAV Sektion Prague in 1883. The hut was named after wealthy Prague businessman Herr Dominikus. At that time, just getting to the upper reaches of the Zamsergrund valley was in itself a major expedition, and the Dominikus Hut provided much-needed accommodation midway before the Schlegeis Project opened up the area almost 100 years later. In 1971 the Schlegeis hydroelectric project was completed, the valley was flooded and the original Dominikus Hut was lost forever. A new privately owned hut was built high above the reservoir with part costs as recompense for loss of the old hut, and it now caters for the many daytime visitors that flock to the area. A journey which 100 years ago would have taken a day's hard slog is now covered in less than an hour by bus from Mayrhofen's railway station.

Proceed NW, climbing steeply, following a good path through forest and alpine rose bushes, zigzagging over blocks along a well-defined trail to a point on the 2300m contour and a footbridge across the **Riepenbach glacial stream**. ▶ Cross the stream and continue to follow the path easily to the **Olperer Hut. A short 3hr**

There is good scenery hereabouts, back across the void towards the Furtschaglhaus, the Grosser Moeseler and the ice wall of the Hochferner and Hochfeiler.

Alternative route to the Olperer Hut
Alternatively, from the Imbis cafe at the car park area and junction of all paths, including the track to Pfitscherjoch, you will find a signpost indicating the way to the Olperer Hut by the Neumarkter Runde Panoramaweg. This route will add an extra hour to the time but scenically it is far more rewarding than the normal route.

Pick up the track as directed, following **Route 535** SW along a well-constructed path through the forest, with rhododendron and dwarf alpine pine bushes, for around 1hr to a **footbridge** across the Unterschrammachbach glacial river at 2127m. Cross the river and follow the track more steeply now NW into the large open combe and glacial basin of Hinterboden (signpost for Pfitscherjochhaus, Geraer Hut and Olperer Hut). **About 1½hr**

Bear right (N) on **Route 502**, better known as the Central Alpine Way, rounding the head of the combe to gain the rocky slopes of Schramerkopf. Follow the obvious rocky trail by traversing around the hillside below Schramerkopf on a path that has been painstakingly laid out, being part paved in places, until its conclusion at the **Olperer Hut**. 3hr

Excellent scenery abounds throughout, particularly in the latter part of the walk, which has exceptional views across the Schlegeis reservoir towards the high peaks.

STAGE 6A
Furtschaglhaus to Olperer Hut via Pfitscherjochhaus

Start	Furtschaglhaus (2295m)
Finish	Olperer Hut (2389m)
Distance	Day 1, 13km; Day 2, 8.5km
Ascent	Day 1, 480m; Day 2, 580m
Descent	Day 1, 300m; Day 2, 400m
Standard time	Day 1, Furtschaglhaus to Pfitscherjochhaus 4–5hr; Day 2, Pfitcherjochhaus to the Olperer Hut 6hr
Note	For maps, see ZRR Stage 6 and Peter Habeler and Olperer Runde Tours Stage 3. After wet weather the streams can be quite ferocious, with the marshy areas being particularly wet. If it's pouring with rain, walkers are advised to take the easy route back down the valley to Schlegeis and from there follow the normal route to the Olperer Hut described in Stage 6

This good alternate route to the Olperer Hut provides some beautiful scenery down the Zamsergrund valley towards Schlegeis and more so once on the Neumarkter Runde Panoramaweg, with its views across the Schlegeisspeicher reservoir. Before vacating the hut, participants who have an interest in war relics should take some time to explore the old army buildings and trench systems just to the south of the Pfitscherjochhaus.

Follow Stage 6 to reach the car park and rest area at Zamsgatterl–Jausenstat. From there pick up the trail for this ancient trading route and follow **Route 524**, the Via Alpina, heading SW along a single-track, graded road that follows the right bank of the Zamserbach river for 5km to **Pfitscherjoch**, the border with Italy and province of Sud Tirol, the Alto Adige and eventually **Pfitscherjochhaus**.

From the Pfitscherjochhaus follow the Peter Habeler Runde Tour, Stage 3. See that route for a full route description.

At the Pfitscherjochhaus

EXCURSION

Ascent of Olperer (3476m) via
Schneegupf south-east ridge

Start	Olperer Hut (2389m)
Distance	6km
Ascent	1100m
Grade	PD
Standard time	Ascent 4–5hr; descent about 3hr

This is an excellent climb over mixed ground with some exhilarating situations on the third-highest peak in the Zillertal, the first ascent of which was made on 10 September 1867 by Paul Grohman, Georg Samer and Gainer Jackl.

Despite the scrappy approach, this fine mountaineering route is full of good alpine situations. The climb itself does not really get going until you reach the rocky platform at the foot of the Schneegupf snowfield: a classic alpine ridge with an airy if somewhat intimidating view across the Olperer's north face. Thereafter, the climb is superb, particularly if you are blessed with good weather. And the scramble over the summit rocks is exciting stuff, with breathtaking scenery tempered with equally breathtaking drops with heaps of exposure.

The near views from the summit, particularly of the rocky Fusstein, are truly superb. While across the void you will see the snow-capped peaks of the Grosser Loeffler, Grosser Moeseler and Hochfeiler. Further to the east, on the far horizon, the Grossvenediger and Grossglockner reveal themselves, while finally to the south are the jagged peaks of the Dolomites. All in all, it is a superb day out!

CAUTIONARY NOTES

For such a popular mountain it is disappointing to note that the main difficulty with this climb is the route finding. First, you need to find your way through the maze of boulders on the upper Riepenkar to get onto the ridge and route proper; you will then have do it again in reverse to get off it.

Thereafter, once on the climb, the difficulties are obvious and well defined. On the snow arête avoid the cornice if there is one, more so early in the season, and on the summit rocks be sure to place running belays at the difficult sections when moving together – all basic mountaineering!

From the hut, the route starts off immediately uphill, heading NW, following a well-defined zigzagging trail in the tracks of the old route to the Geraer Hut via the Alpeiner Scharte on Route 502 (Central Alpine Way). ▶

Continue through the **Riepenkar couloir**, heading for the intersection with the track over the snow slopes of the now dormant Riepenkees glacier to the Spannagelhaus (signpost for the Olperer). **½hr**

At this intersection, continue as before for another ¾hr, making a rising traverse, bearing left (W) through difficult ground of large blocks and boulders, where route finding is not always obvious. Look out for stone

This route was redirected in 2006 due to severe earth tremors that resulted in massive rockfalls to the east of the Alpeiner Scharte, making the route unsafe.

Climbing the Olperer (3476m)

Schneegupf

Olperer Hut

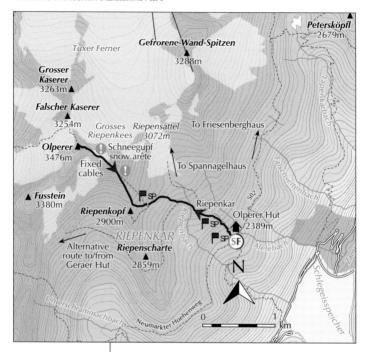

cairns, but generally head for a notch on the south ridge immediately above the Riepenkarscharte at point 2864m on the lower section of the Riepengrat ridge coming down from Olperer's south ridge (signpost for the Olperer). **1–1¼hr**

Pick a way through the rocks, scrambling over difficult mixed ground of large boulders and patches of snow, heading in a northerly direction with the simple objective of getting onto the ridge. There are some stone cairns in places, but these are neither frequent nor obvious with the result that there are quite a few false trails. Once on the ridge, continue to climb, following the natural line of the ridge, turning left or right over difficult sections. The ridge is guarded at its head by a much-steeper rock outcrop. Scramble through the rocks of the head wall, which leads eventually to a platform-cum-terrace on the lower edge of the **Schneegupf snowfield**. **1hr** This is good place for a short break and a recce of the route, as the summit is clearly seen from here. ▶

From here on, the route is pretty obvious. Climb the steep snowfield and head for the snow arête and ridge on the northern skyline, keeping left on the south side if the ridge is corniced; otherwise, climb the ridge direct. Continue along the snow crest, heading for the rocks coming down from the summit. Here there are excellent views across the Olperer's northern flank to the Gefrorene-Wand-Spitzen with its attendant summer ski slopes and the great bulk of the rocky Fusstein (3380m), even if it is something of a slag heap.

Traverse around the base of the rocks to gain a chimney fitted out with **fixed cables**, spikes and staples to aid your passage. Clip into the gear provided and climb the chimney direct to gain the ridge. Continue along the ridge – very exposed in places – climbing the rocks until stopped by a tower just below the summit. Gingerly bypass the tower on the right (N) and exit over a small, narrow snowfield to gain the somewhat small summit of the **Olperer** with its sculpted metal cross. **2hr**

In descent the route has to be reversed in its entirety. This demands a little extra care when passing the rock tower

Excellent scenery opens up across the whole of the Zillertal and the near peaks of the Olperer and Fusstein.

Climbing through the fixed wires on the summit ridge

and down climbing the rock chimney; for a group of people it is quicker to rig an abseil rope.

Similarly, when descending the steepish snow arête, when the snow will be less than ideal, climbers should keep themselves reasonably well spaced out to check a fall should the need arise. **About 3hr**

STAGE 7
Olperer Hut to Friesenberghaus

Start	Olperer Hut (2389m)
Finish	Friesenberghaus (2498m)
Distance	4km
Ascent	290m
Descent	200m
Standard time	2½–3hr

While somewhat short in duration, this very pleasant half-day outing has excellent views across the valley towards Schlegeis and, a little later, to the triangular wedge of the Hoher Riffler. Traversing high above the Zamsergrund valley, the route has excellent scenery throughout.

The view from opposite the hut with its tiny alpine lake makes for a strong contrast, with the bulk of the Hoher Riffler being particularly impressive.

CAUTIONARY NOTES

This is a very straightforward walk. However, a degree of care needs to be exercised when descending the gully system and rock buttress that overlooks the hut and Friesenbergsee. Obviously, this is made more problematic when patches of snow linger on the rock ledges and steep sections. Those who are not entirely sure-footed should stay close to a companion for assistance and make good use of those trekking poles.

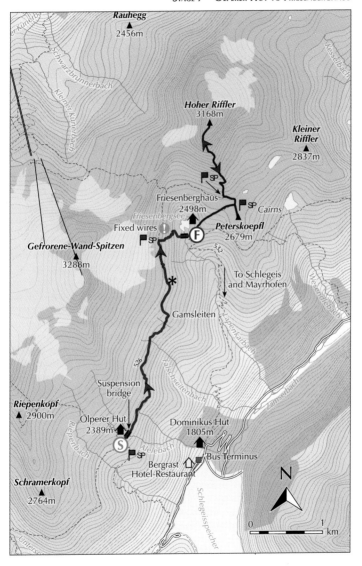

111

From the hut, with the signpost just outside the front door, follow **Route 526** on the ZRR. The route starts off on a good track where after 5min or so you will reach a **suspension bridge** over a washed-out gully, lasting evidence of the rockfall and mud avalanche that tore the back off the hut in 1998 in one single destructive stroke; this forced the hut to close for a season and perhaps sealed the fate of this fine old hut. Thereafter, the route traverses rocks and grassy slopes on a good gentle path, generally on the 2500m contour, bypassing the Gefrorene-Wand-Spitzen's east flank and the rocks of the **Gamsleiten**.

Once past the Gamsleiten, the path makes a rising traverse N, which eventually leads to a junction with a high-level track leading to the clearly visible Friesenbergscharte at 2912m (**signpost**). 1½hr ◄

Excellent views extend towards the peak of the Hoher Riffler. Those with sharp eyes will be able to pick out many of the stone cairns on top of the little peak of Peterskoepfl.

At a point overlooking the hut and Friesenbergsee, descend E, with care, down a steep, rocky gully system in a series of zigzags over awkward sloping rock ledges. This area is frequently snow covered early in season, with patches of snow remaining throughout the summer.

Thereafter, continue to descend the Uramentenloch rock buttress until the ground naturally eases at the small alpine lake of the Friesenbergsee just below the hut.

Cross the **footbridge** and reascend easy slopes to the historic **Friesenberghaus**. **1hr**

EXCURSION
Ascent of Hoher Riffler (3168m)

Start	Friesenberghaus (2498m)
Distance	4km
Ascent	750m
Grade	F-
Standard time	Ascent 3½hr; descent 2½hr
Note	For map, see Stage 7

If you leave early from the Olperer Hut, the Hoher Riffler will provide an interesting afternoon excursion. The summit has excellent views in all directions, particularly so across the Gefrorene-Wand-Spitzen, the Olperer and the peaks of Hintertux.

The route climbs the south-east ridge and is characterised by a series of buttresses or humps, and while the route has been re-marked in recent years, there is still plenty of opportunity for false trails, particularly if the route is partly snow covered.

CAUTIONARY NOTES

Since the route is mainly over rocks with patches of snow, most of the difficulties are obvious and require nothing more than common sense and basic mountaineering skills.

However, special attention needs to be exercised in the mid to upper sections of the climb, both in ascent and descent, as the route is quite steep and very exposed in places, particularly on the summit ridge overlooking the summer ski slopes of the Gefrorene-Wand-Spitzen.

Otherwise, this is a very pleasant excursion with few difficulties that should be within the capabilities of all participants undertaking the Zillertal Rucksack Route.

From the hut proceed N (signpost) for a short distance then turn NE up and over rocks and boulders, heading in the direction of an obvious col at the foot of the Hoher Riffler's south ridge and junction with the line of cliffs that form the Wesendleskar Schneide ridge and the satellite peak of **Peterskoepfl** (2679m) (**signpost**). ½hr

From the col at 2628m, head NW, keeping left of the Riffler's south ridge where, after a short distance, you will reach a **signpost** indicating the way up the mountain. Turn right, and continue N, zigzagging up a well-laid-out rocky staircase-type trail to the top of the first hump or step on the south ridge. **1hr**

The route now steepens, zigzagging to and fro across difficult ground, over and around large boulders and blocks – be observant and watch out as the way ahead is not always obvious. A further ½hr leads to a small plateau and the top of the second hump, which happens to be ideal for a photo stop. Continue along the ridge, crossing patches of snow to exit, where you are confronted by a steep rock buttress; pass this on the right, which is quite exposed. Continue to follow the line of the arête of the buttress to emerge on top of the third hump. **1hr**

From here on, the route steepens another few degrees to emerge on the ridge overlooking the Tuxerfernerhaus cable-car station. Hug the mountain, as parts of the ridge are very exposed with some sizeable drops. Continue along the ridge, crossing permanent snow cover on the 3000m contour, heading for a low point on the south-east ridge. Scramble up steep rocks to gain the ridge proper. Thereafter, follow the obvious ridge line over rocks with patches of snow to the summit of **Hoher Riffler** (3168m) with its large metal cross. **1hr** This last section offers some excellent mountaineering situations, being very exposed in places and quite airy with some astonishing drops!

The **view** from the summit is extensive in all directions; it's a summit from which you can see all four of Austria's highest peaks. The immediate view lies across the void to the Gefrorene-Wand-Spitzen cable-car station. This leads the eye to the near

Looking towards the Friesenbergscharte with the Olperer in the far distance

horizon and the triangular wedge and bulk of the Olperer. Further afield, to the south and south-east, are the Hochfeiler massif and the Italian Dolomites beyond. To the east Austria's highest mountain, the Grossglockner, stands proud with the well-defined snowy ridge of the Grossvenediger (4th). To the west are the mountains of the Oetztal and Stubai Alps, the Schrankogel, the Weisskugel (3rd) and the Wildspitze (2nd) all being clearly visible. Lastly, to the north lie the limestone peaks of the Karwendel and the Zugspitze in neighbouring

Germany. And last, for anyone undertaking either the Peter Habeler Runde or the Olperer Runde Tours, the summit provides you with an opportunity to scan and recce the route across the Friesenbergscharte and on past Spannagelhaus and all the way to Tuxerjochhaus.

In descent from the summit, retrace your tracks, exercising a little more caution as you pass through the very steep, loose bouldery slopes of the mid section until easier ground is reached at the col of the Peterskoepfl scharte. **2hr** This a good place to recce the route to the Friesenbergscharte before returning to the hut. ½**hr**

EXCURSION
Ascent of Peterskoepfl (2679m)

Start	Friesenberghaus (2498m)
Distance	2km
Ascent	200m
Grade	F- (an easy walk)
Standard time	Ascent ¾hr; descent ½hr
Note	For map, see Stage 7

This is a first-class short excursion, ideal for a picnic and for those who aspire to be sculptors or would-be stone masons.

From the hut, follow the route description for the Hoher Riffler as far as the col below the Riffler's south ridge. At the col, turn right and head S along a vague trail on the craggy cliffs of the Wesendleskar Schneide ridge, then scramble up rocks immediately below the summit of **Peterskoepfl**. ¾**hr**

The summit plateau is littered with stone cairns of every perceivable description, many of which defy the rules of gravity; they are all said to represent those souls lost to the holocaust in World War 2.

There are excellent views across the whole of the Zillertal. The Hochfeiler, Berliner Spitze and the snowy slopes of the Schwarzenstein are all easy to identify, while those with the ultimate sharp eyes will be able to locate the Berliner Hut at the head of the Zemmgrund valley.

Return by the same route, enjoying great scenery towards the Hoher Riffler and the Friesenbergscharte, as well as elevated views of the hut itself. ½**hr**

On Peterskoepfl, looking towards the Schwarzenstein and the Berliner Hut

STAGE 8
Friesenberghaus to Gams Hut

Start	Friesenberghaus (2498m)
Finish	Gams Hut (1916m)
Distance	13.5km
Ascent	About 600m
Descent	1100m
Standard time	10–12hr

This final stage takes you from the highest hut in the Zillertal to the lowest. But don't let that statement fool you into thinking the route is all downhill – it isn't! While the route is very long, there are excellent views of the valleys and main Zillertal peaks, and in early summer the trail is well decorated with alpine flowers, including a profusion of pink alpine rose bushes in many places.

Official timings for the connection between the huts are 7 to 8 hours from Friesenberghaus and 8 to 9 hours in the opposite direction, from the Gams Hut. Unless you are tip-top fit, these times are woefully inadequate and it is unlikely you would cover the distance and terrain involved. More realistic times are 10 to 12 hours from the Friesenberghaus and 12 hours from the Gams Hut.

The route is long and serious, although not as demanding in mountaineering terms as the Karl von Edel Hut–Kasseler Hut connection. It is, however, unsuitable for novices and definitely not a route to undertake in poor weather, although there are ample opportunities to get off the route and descend into the valley should the need arise.

The route traverses up and down roughly on the 2000m contour high above the Zamsergrund valley, taking in its entire length. Should participants be blessed with good weather, the route has excellent scenery throughout, from the ice and rock at Friesenberghaus to the pretty, high alpine pastures at Pitzenalm and Feldalm.

The route is also superb for plants and animals, being home to chamois, as well as marmots, eagles and countless varieties of alpine flowers, particularly alpine rose bushes and martagon lilies.

CAUTIONARY NOTES

The route's main difficulty is its length, followed by a more subtle problem of route finding, which is not always obvious when the trail is overgrown with vegetation and the visibility is poor.

Needless to say, this is not a route to undertake in less than favourable weather.

Be on your way early and out of the hut for 06:00; having breakfast en route will ensure you arrive at the Gams Hut before dark.

The route can be split into four distinct sections:

Friesenberghaus (2498m) to Kesselalm (2006m), 4hr
From the hut, Route 530 contours E around and across the ridge coming down from Peterskoepfl, affording the last and perhaps best view of the hut before it is consigned to memory. Thereafter, descend broken ground to a signpost pointing the way to the Gams Hut and the descent route to Breitlahner. The route now continues as **Route 536**, heading NE past a small lake, **Wesendlkarsee**

Fabulous scenery looking towards the Berliner Hut

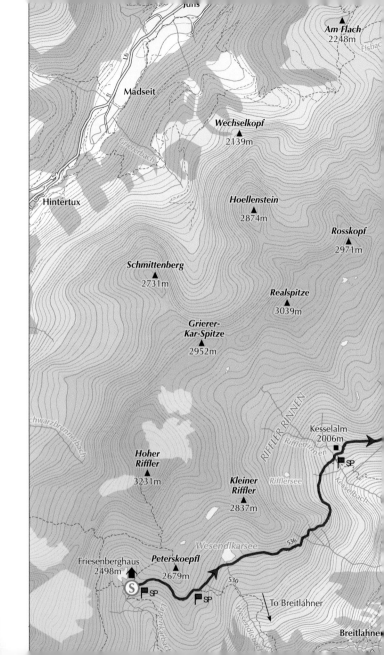

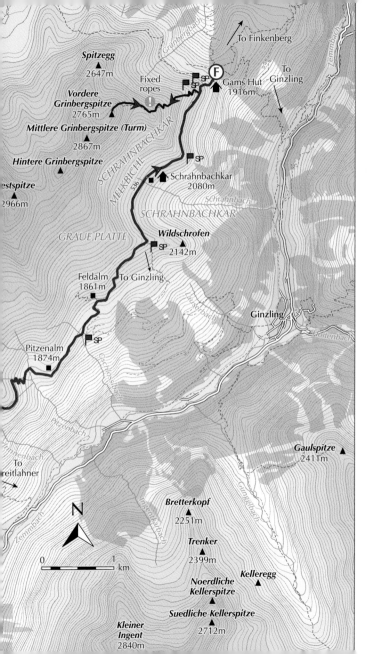

Crossing the many streams at the Kesselalm

It is the ascent of these slopes that adds the time when coming from the Gams Hut.

(2375m), and ascending slightly over a boulder-strewn slope below the Schoenlahner Kopf.

This type of ground is interesting but demands close attention. Watch out for chamois (*gemsbock*) on the lower slopes, as this area now supports a sizeable herd of this small alpine antelope. Continue as before in a NE direction, then more N under the crags of the Riffler Rinnen gully which eventually give way as the route continues in a zigzag descent to a footbridge and the tiny alm at **Kesselalm** (2006m) (signpost). ◀

This is a first-class place for a rest and a drink, with entertaining views along the Zemmgrund valley and across the void to the Berliner Hut.

Kesselalm (2006m) to Pitzenalm (1874m), 2hr

Having descended into the open combe that forms the Birglberg Kar, you will have to regain lost height by ascending grassy slopes for 100m to reach the 2100m contour. The route now crosses two spurs before descending through unpleasant vegetated slopes that can prove problematic as the path is frequently wet and slippery. Continue through fields to **Pitzenalm** (1874m), where provided the *Bauer* (farmer) or *Jager* (huntsman) is in residence, refreshments may be available (signpost). ▶

Pitzenalm (1874m) to Graue Platte (2177m), 2hr
From the delightful Pitzenalm the track continues NE along the 1800m contour, passing through the trees of the high alp to emerge at **Feldalm** (1861m). From here the track makes a rising traverse NE to Graue Platte, first passing through dwarf pine trees, followed by boulder fields, to the small col that forms the **Graue Platte** (2177m) (**signpost**). The scenery is excellent hereabouts, particularly the view up the Gunggl valley leading up to the prominent Zsigmondyspitze. There is also a further opportunity to descend to Ginzling should the need arise.

Graue Platte (2177m) to the Gams Hut (1916m), 2hr
After reaching the col of the Graue Platte, the route descends steeply into the broad combe of Melkbichl, where many streams congregate (good place for flowers), crossing more broken ground to reach the tiny alm of **Schrahnbachkar** (2080m). From here the route heads NE then N up and down through boulders, scrub forest and on typical alpine paths before making a zigzag descent off the ridge coming down from the Grinbergspitze to the **Gams Hut** (1916m) with its bright copper roof.

This is roughly the halfway point on the route. Those who are not faring too well should perhaps consider descending to Ginzling.

EXCURSION
Ascent of Vordere Grinbergspitze (2765m)

Start	Gams Hut (1916m)
Distance	4km
Ascent	825m
Grade	F
Standard time	Ascent 3hr; descent about 1½hr
Note	For map, see Stage 8

Unfortunately, the Gams Hut is very much a one-mountain hut. Despite this drawback, an ascent of the Vordere Grinbergspitze is a worthy excursion on snow-free rock, and it offers some very good scenery. The mountain dominates the head of the valley above Mayrhofen and comprises three summits: the Vordere, Mittlere and Hintere, respectively the fore summit, middle summit and summit beyond. The route described goes only as far as the Vordere, as the route over the Mittlere and Hintere is a more serious undertaking and beyond the scope of these notes.

The highlight of the route is without doubt the rock garden, which provides some excellent scrambling and some good photo opportunities.

Once on the summit, the views are extensive, although the mighty snow-capped peaks which have become so familiar to us have now receded to the far horizon, making way for lesser-known peaks above Finkenberg and Mayrhofen.

CAUTIONARY NOTES

The only area that requires close attention is the section through and around the massive boulders in the rock garden and the rocks close to the summit.

From the summit you may be tempted to cross the linking ridge to the Mittlere Grinbergspitze, in which case please re-read my comments in the introduction above before making your decision.

From the Gams Hut, retrace your steps along the path of **Route 536**, heading W to join the junction of the track leading to the Graue Platte (signpost for Grinbergspitze and Friesenberghaus). **½hr**

Continue W up easy zigzags, through alpine rose bushes, to join the main ridge proper coming down from Vordere Grinbergspitze. At this point, a crucifix cross is clearly visible across the void on the Spitzegg (2647m). **1hr**

From here on, the route becomes more serious and exposed as the steepness of the ridge increases. The route continues to zigzag through broken ground and a rock garden of giant house-sized boulders, providing interesting scrambling requiring four points of contact with the rock on the more demanding sections, which are aided by fixed wires and metal staples. Hereabouts there is excellent scenery, particularly the rough and tumble of the house-sized boulders, but also look out for chamois and marmots which also reside in the area; the shrill warning whistle of the marmots will be heard breaking the silence.

At approximately 2700m the summit cross on the **Vordere Grinbergspitze** becomes clearly visible, making an obvious target for the final pull up to the summit. **1–1½hr**

Spectacular scenery amid house-sized boulders in the rock garden

As noted earlier, the continuation of the route to the Mittlere and Hintere is beyond the scope of these notes. My advice is to stay put at the first summit. However, for those of you who are curious and may be tempted to go and have a look, particularly when the interconnecting ridge between the Vordere and Mittlere is snow free, the connecting ridge has some good, interesting Grade II climbing. The route from the Mittlere to the Hintere requires the use of ropes, having a rock-climbing Grade of IV.

Descend by reversing the same route. You should have sufficient time in the afternoon to descend to Ginzling, Finkenberg and Mayrhofen if that is your wish. If not, salute your achievement and enjoy your evening in the *Gemuetlichkeit* (homely) tradition and charm of the **Gams Hut**. About 1½hr

STAGE 9
Gams Hut to Ginzling and Mayrhofen

Start	Gams Hut (1916m)
Finish	Mayrhofen town (633m)
Distance	7km
Ascent	Negligible; all downhill
Descent	950m, then bus thereafter from Ginzling to Mayrhofen
Standard time	3hr

This is the first option of a choice of routes to end the Zillertal Rucksack Route Tour. The route descends through some very pleasant forest scenery to end in Ginzling, one of the most charming villages in the Zillertal.

The path descends the Georg-Herholz-Weg in a continuation of the east-to-west ridge coming down from the Grinbergspitze. The track then enters a

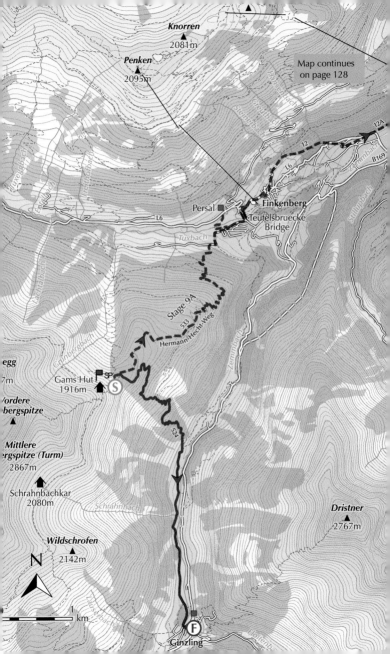

Knorren
2081m

Penken
2095m

Map continues
on page 128

12A

12

L6

B169

Persal

Finkenberg

Teufelsbruecke
Bridge

L6

Tuxbach

Stage 9A

533

Hermann-Hecht-Weg

Gams Hut
1916m ⓢ

egg
7m

Vordere
bergspitze

Mittlere
ergspitze (Turm)
2867m

Schrahnbachkar
2080m

524

Dristner
2767m

Wildschrofen
2142m

Schrahnbach

N

1
km

Ⓕ
Ginzling

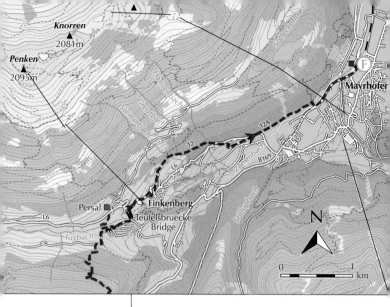

woodland environment with several pleasant alpine glades, descending in a series of zigzags, some of which are quite steep and slippery when wet.

Once on the valley floor the quiet of the forest is broken as the path continues through farmland to a bridge at **Schrahnbach** over the loud roar of the Zemmbach river. For participants who do not wish to end the tour at Ginzling, there is a bus stop for Mayrhofen by the bridge. **About 2hr**

Otherwise, continue to follow the path along the left bank of the river. Unfortunately, the track is avalanche prone and not always open; if it is closed, there will be a *Gesprutt* sign to say the route is temporarily closed and that walkers should follow the path on and off at the side of the road into **Ginzling**. **1hr**

A lunch stop is highly recommended at the Alte Ginzling Hotel, for the best fresh trout in the Zillertal, before continuing by bus to end the tour in **Mayrhofen**.

The timetable for Bus 4102 from Ginzling to Mayrhofen is as follows:

09:59/10:29/10:59/11:29 and every half hour thereafter.

STAGE 9A
Gams Hut to Finkenberg and Mayrhofen

Start	Gams Hut (1916m)
Finish	Mayrhofen town (633m)
Distance	10km
Ascent	Negligible; all downhill
Descent	1030m to Finkenberg; 1260m to Mayrhofen
Standard time	2hr to Finkenberg plus 1hr to Mayrhofen
Note	For map, see Stage 9

The second option of the choice of routes to end the Zillertal Rucksack Route Tour is an equally pleasant walk, perhaps more of a stroll, through very pleasant forest of spruce and larch with the added attraction of visiting the very old Teufelsbruecke.

From the hut, descend NE across the pleasant slopes of the Gamsberg on **Route 533**, then more steeply down through the forest following the Hermann-Hecht-Weg, losing 600m of height. At the foot of the Nesselwang (1305m), the route turns W, descending over alpine pastures to enter the tiny village of **Finkenberg** at its western edge. **2hr** Here you will find signs for Teufelsbruecke, the gravity-defying Devil's Bridge over the Tuxbach river and Route 12A into Mayrhofen. Those with time on their hands and energy to spare can walk into Mayrhofen. **1hr**

For those of you who may wish to dine in Finkenberg at one of the pleasant hotels before finally taking the bus to **Mayrhofen**, the timetable for Bus 4104 from Finkenberg (Persal) to Mayrhofen is as follows: 09:20/09:55/10:55/11:55/12:55 and every half hour thereafter.

PETER HABELER AND OLPERER RUNDE TOURS

Approaching the alpine ponds and redundant border control buildings at Pfitscherjoch (Stage 2)

At Pfitscherjoch Haus (PHRT Stage 2)

What's in a name? Because the tours are very similar, some explanation is necessary to clarify the subtle differences.

The Olperer Runde Tour is essentially a tour that falls within the territory of Austria and has been in existence from the mid 1960s when animosity still prevailed between Austria and Italy over the vexed question of sovereignty along the border with Italy and the Sud Tirol (South Tirol): the territory annexed from Austria to Italy as war reparations at the Treaty of St-Germain in 1919 following World War 1.

The route for the Olperer Runde Tour is, as the name suggests, a circular tour around the Olperer, the third-highest peak in the Zillertal and the highest mountain totally within the Zillertal. The route started at the Geraer Hut in the Valsertal, then crossed the high alpine pass of the Alpeiner Scharte to the Olperer Hut and onto the Friesenberghaus, before turning W to cross the Friesenbergscharte to the Tuxerjochhaus, turning and coming full circle to return to the Geraer Hut.

Around 2012, to honour Peter Habeler's 70th birthday, the most famous of Austria's and the Zillertal's mountaineers, the Olperer Runde Tour was extended to embrace two huts on the Italian side of the Sud Tirol border with Austria, namely the Landshuter Europa Hut (Rifugio Europa) and Pfitscherjochhaus (Rifugio Passo di Vizze). Both these huts were occupied by the Italian military for many years until Austria joined the European Union in 1995, when all border restrictions were removed.

Essentially the Olperer Runde Tour remains as it always has been, whereas the Peter Habeler Runde Tour now includes the two Italian huts as mentioned above.

Both tours can be undertaken in either direction, although it is recommended that you undertake the tour counterclockwise to avoid the difficult ascents of the high passes to the Alpeiner Scharte and Friesenbergscharte, respectively.

TREK 2
Peter Habeler Runde

Start	Touristenrast Gasthof
Finish	Touristenrast Gasthof
Distance	53.5km
Ascent	3570m
Descent	3720m
Time	7 days
Excursions	Hoher Riffler, Peterskoepfl

While the official leaflet published by the tourist information offices of Mayrhofen, Wipptal and Sterzing states that the Runde Tour may be started at any of the main valley villages or huts, the author's recommendation is to start and finish the tour at the Touristenrast Gasthof at the head of the Valsertal valley, undertaking the Peter Habeler Runde Tour as follows: Touristenrast Gasthof to Landshuter Europa Hut, then to Pfitscherjochhaus, Olperer Hut, Friesenberghaus, Tuxerjochhaus, Geraer Hut and finishing back at Touristenrast Gasthof. Similarly, this follows for the Olperer Runde Tour, but leaving out the two Italian huts.

For the Peter Habeler Runde Tour, this provides a continuous tour of seven days staying in six huts and a total distance of 53.5km while ascending and descending some 3600m through stunning scenery and, at times, very challenging terrain.

See www.mayrhofen.at/en/stories/peter-habeler-route
- Stage 1 Touristenrast Gasthof to Landshuter Europa Hut 5–6hr
- Stage 2 Landshuter Europa Hut to Pfitscherjochhaus 3–4hr
- Stage 3 Pfitscherjochhaus to Olperer Hut 5hr
- Stage 4 Olperer Hut to Friesenberghaus 2½–3hr
- Stage 5 Friesenberghaus to Tuxerjochhaus via Friesenbergscharte 6–7hr

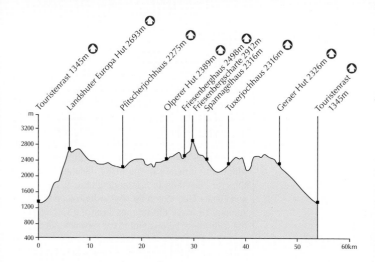

- Stage 6 Tuxerjochhaus to Geraer Hut 6–7hr
- Stage 7 Geraer Hut to Touristenrast Gasthof 2½–3hr

Getting to the start

From Innsbruck railway station, take the regional train to Steinach am Brenner, a small town on the Austrian side of the Brenner pass. Trains depart at 09:22/10:22/11:22.

Should you have to stay overnight in Steinach, the Hotel Zur Rose is recommended as an alternative start and finish point to Innsbruck (see Appendix A).

From the railway station in Steinach, take the local Postbus service, by the railway station, to Touristenrast Gasthof at the head of the Valsertal valley, a journey time of just short of 1hr. Be aware that there is no overnight accommodation at Touristenrast, which is a shame as it would be a great place to stay.

The 4144 bus is a limited service, departing daily at 11:47/13:47. Note there is no bus service on a Sunday, but there is a local taxi service: Wipptal Taxi 0043 664 122 3055 or email info@wipptaltaxi.at

This part of the tour to Touristenrast is shared with Stage 1 of the Zillertal South Tirol Tour and Stage 1 of the Olperer Runde Tour.

Starting from Mayrhofen

For those wishing to undertake the Peter Habeler Runde Tour from the Zillertal valley, from Mayrhofen, you can start the tour at the Pfitscherjochhaus (see Hut Directory and follow the Day Walk itinerary details of how to get to Pfitscherjochhaus), thus omitting the start from Touristenrast Gasthof in the Valsertal valley and the trek to the Landshuter Europa Hut. From Pfitscherjochhaus follow the itinerary of the PHRT, heading first to the Olperer Hut, then to Friesenberghaus, Tuxerjochhaus and Geraer Hut, to end the tour at Touristenrast Gasthof. Attempt to make the journey from the Geraer Hut to the Landshuter Europa Hut is not recommended, as the route is exceedingly long – around 10 hours. Should you have to return to the Zillertal valley, follow the itinerary for Stage 2 of the Zillertal South Tirol Tour to the glacial ponds at Hinterboden, then the well-marked trail back to Schlegeis and the bus service to Mayrhofen.

STAGE 1
Touristenrast Gasthof to Landshuter Europa Hut

Start	Touristenrast Gasthof (1345m)
Finish	Landshuter Europa Hut (2693m)
Distance	8km
Ascent	1300m
Descent	About 100m
Standard time	5–6hr
Note	See 'Getting to the start' for information about getting to Touristenrast. There is no overnight accommodation at Touristenrast

What could be better than starting your tour at the tiny farmstead hamlet of Touristenrast, full of colour and Tirolean charm. Despite the obvious charm, do not linger here too long as a full day of serious trekking lies ahead.

As the first day of the tour, the route is quite demanding, taking in 1300m of height while negotiating some quite challenging ground. Apart from the easy charm of Touristenrast Gasthof and Helga's Alm, the forest section offers little in terms of mountain scenery. This changes once the route enters the Stierkar boulder field, but here the scenery remains thwarted by the sheer scale of the Kraxentrager and adjacent peaks until the final climb to the Lange Wand, which will challenge your ability as you negotiate the various fixed aids of pegs, staples and a ladder crossing the ridge. Here the route opens out to almost 360-degree stunning scenery, particularly towards the west across the Wipptal and the mountains of the Stubai Alps.

The challenge continues along the rocks to the Sumpfschartl, which give way to marginally easier ground to the strategically located Landshuter Europa Hut. Straddling the Austrian-Italian border, and the demarcation of the Nord and Sud Tirol, the hut overlooks the great void towards the Zillertal Alps, to what remains of the hanging glaciers of the Hochferner, and down into the long Pfitchertal valley and across the Brenner pass, deep into Italy and the Alto Adige, all of which make this a brilliant day out in the mountains and a fitting way to start the Peter Habeler Runde Tour. Enjoy!

CAUTIONARY NOTES

While the standard time is given as 5hr, 6hr is more realistic due to the 1300m of ascent. The most difficult part of the route is crossing the steep, broken ground between Aussere Zeischalm and Sumpfschartl, which involves over 600m of ascent through boulders.

This route is best avoided in less than favourable weather. See below for bad weather alternatives.

From Touristenrast Gasthof guest house, walk down the road for 100 metres or so to a roadside shrine. Turn left at the signpost for Nockeralm (better known locally as Helga's Alm) and Route 529 and follow the forest service road SE, first for the short distance to **Helga's Alm** (refreshments available), then for approximately 1¼km, climbing steadily on the Geistbeckweg, until you reach some hairpin bends (**signpost**).

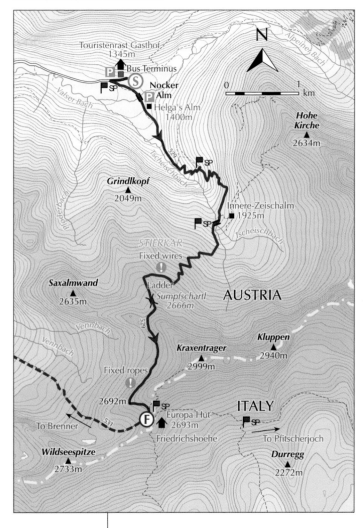

Leave the road and follow the trail into the forest, climbing steeply for approximately 500m along the

zigzag path until you reach a small clearing with a crucifix cross. **1–1½hr**

The route now turns more S, traversing through the forest, crossing a number of streams, some with bridges, until you reach open countryside at **Innere Zeischalm**, on the 1925m contour. Here you enter the huge Tscheischalpe amphitheatre of mountains, which is dominated by the Sagwandpitze, the Hohe Wand and the Kraxentrager (the witch's beam.) ▶ (**Signpost**)

Continue as before, climbing steadily now to gain 600m of height over the steep, rocky ground of the sparsely marked Stierkar boulder field, heading for some imposing-looking cliffs aptly named the Lange Wand, the long wall.

Here is a good place to deploy your improvised harness, as the ground steepens considerably near the top, with the route protected and assisted by metal pegs and **fixed cables**; the most difficult section has a short ladder to gain a notch in the ridge. **2hr** ▶

Cross to the west side of the Lange Wand ridge, progressing S over easier rocky ground with **fixed wires** to the little **Sumpfschartl col** at 2666m. **1hr** From here great views stretch across the Wipptal valley to the Stubai Alps.

The route as seen from Nocker Alm, looking towards Zeischalm and the obvious col of the Pfitscherscharte

This is a good place to take a break.

This is a great situation with brilliant scenery, if somewhat airy and exposed, but not a place to dwell in iffy weather.

From here on, descend a little on the zigzag trail and then cross the open boulder field ahead (S) below the headwall of the Kraxentrager, heading over easier broken ground for 1km to reach a small col at **2692m**. From this point, the Landshuter Europa Hut starts to come into view. **1hr**

Cross the obvious rocky ground ahead to reach the magnificently sited **Landshuter Europa Hut** (2693m), the highest hut of the Peter Habeler Runde Tour. **½hr**

Bad weather options

The forest streams at Zeischalm can be quite difficult after a spell of rain, not to mention the route-finding difficulties crossing the Stierkar boulder field. In the event of bad weather, you could consider taking the alternative, less-demanding route to the hut via Brennersee and the Venntal valley as follows:

Take the regional train from Innsbruck to Brenner railway station, on the border with Italy and the Sud Tirol.

From Brenner railway station, walk down the road for 1km in the direction of Brennersee and Innsbruck. ◀ After about 15min you will come to a road underpass with signs for Venntal. Cross under the roads, then follow the single-track road until it comes to a natural conclusion at a group of farm buildings and barns with a signpost pointing the way for Route 531 and the Landshuter Europa Hut.

From the barns, the route climbs steadily through the forest, overgrown in parts, until it emerges on the edge of a large boulder-strewn, amphitheatre-type corrie. Continue SE, following the gradual rocky trail, parts of which are nicely paved and laid out, a reminder that this was the work of military engineers. About 1km from the hut, the trail gets steeper, zigzagging to the little col just below the **Landshuter Europa Hut**. **4hr**

A further alternative is to miss out the Landshuter Europa Hut and follow Stage 1 and 2 of the Zillertal South Tirol Tour to Pfitscherjochhaus.

Be careful here as the roads are very busy.

STAGE 2
Landshuter Europa Hut to Pfitscherjochhaus

Start	Landshuter Europa Hut (2693m)
Finish	Pfitscherjochhaus (2275m)
Distance	7.5km
Ascent	About 250m
Descent	650m
Standard time	3–4hr

A very pleasant alpine walk that walks through history, with some exceptionally fine scenery.

From the Landshuter Europa Hut progress N on a paved path to a little col, then turn E as the route joins the **Tiroler Hoehenweg** and **Landshuter Hoehenweg** (sign-post for Route 528).

The main observation is that of the well-engineered **path** left by the Italian military engineers. It was

Remnants of the military road, looking towards the peaks of the Hochfeiler

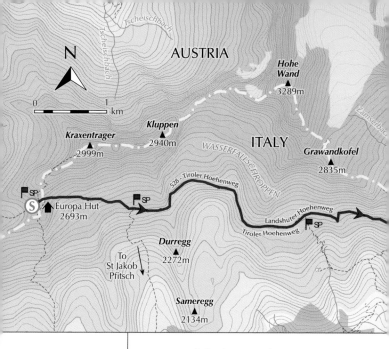

constructed after the Treaty of St-Germain in 1919, when both the North and South Tirol were occupied by the Italian military. At that time, the Landshuter Hut had a strategic advantage with commanding views towards the Brenner pass and south across huge swathes of the Sud Tirol. The path, therefore, needed to be militarised so that supplies could be effectively transported by men and mules from the main garrison at Pfitscherjoch, as the Italians were fearful that Austria would invade Italy along the border to reclaim their beloved Sud Tirol.

Military concerns aside, this is a very good alpine promenade with fine scenery towards the main peaks of the Zillertal, particularly the Hochfeiler. Enjoy!

From the col, descend the rocky trail where after about 1km you will reach a signpost pointing down the valley to the Sud Tirol towns of St Jakob and Pfitsch. After

To the
Olperer
Hut

Border Control
and Chapel

(F)

cherjochhaus
2275m

ochplatte
2100m

a further short distance you will reach a second col from where the scenery and general panorama towards the high peaks of the Zillertal start to reveal themselves, particularly the obvious bulk of the Hochferner. **1hr**

From the col, continue around the head of the *Wasserfallkofel* (waterfall bowl), where many streams congregate, hence the name, for roughly 1km, between the 2200 and 2400m contours. ▶ Progress around the rocky slopes of the **Wasserfallschroppen**, no doubt named because the hillside bleeds water.

Continue E for about 2km on the well-laid-out rocky path, from where the Pfitscherjochhaus is visible on its rocky knoll across the void, until you reach the small Nusserkopf rocky outcrop at 2354m. ▶ **1hr**

Here you will start to notice that the trail has been very well paved with large rocky slabs, reminders of the endeavours and hard work of the army engineers.

There are excellent views towards the main peaks of the Zillertal.

From here on, the path descends gradually towards Pfitscherjoch proper, first to the alpine tarn of **Jochsee** and then to the broad Pfitscherjoch itself with the abandoned **border police control building** and **chapel**. Excellent views extend down the valley into Austria, towards the Olperer, Schlegeis and Mayrhofen. **1hr**

To the south is a large sign that welcomes you to Italy and the Alto Adige province, better known as the Sud Tirol, then after a short walk up the hill you will be welcomed at the very substantial **Pfitscherjochhaus**. ½hr

STAGE 3
Pfitscherjochhaus to Olperer Hut

Start	Pfitscherjochhaus (2275m)
Finish	Olperer Hut (2389m)
Distance	8.5km
Ascent	580m
Descent	400m
Standard time	5–6hr

This very good alternative route to the Olperer Hut provides some excellent scenery down the Zamsergrund valley towards Schlegeis, then offers more from the Neumarkter Runde Panoramaweg, with fabulous views across the Schlegeisspeicher hydroelectric reservoir to the snow-capped peaks of Hochfeiler and Grosser Moeseler. Before vacating, participants who have an interest in war relics should take some time to explore the old army buildings and trench systems just to the south of the Pfitscherjochhaus.

CAUTIONARY NOTES

The standard time for the route is given as 5hr but this is rarely achieved, 6hr being more realistic.

As already implied, the route is generally a fine-weather route but be cautious if the weather turns *Kaiser Wetter* (weather fit for a king) and perfect after a spell of rain, as the marshy ground at Stampler Boden gets easily flooded, and the other glacial stream becomes difficult to cross, with raging torrents that will sweep you off your feet.

In really poor weather the best option is to walk to Schlegeis and follow the easier trail to the Olperer Hut, as per ZRR Stage 6, or stay overnight at the very comfortable Dominikus Hut.

From Pfitscherjochhaus walk down the service road and return to the border crossing, passed the previous day, to the old **border police customs hut** and road side **chapel**.

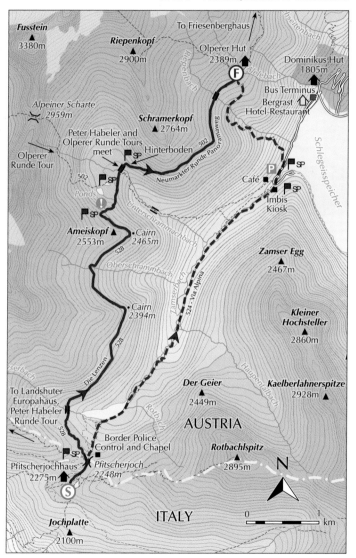

*At the head of the
Zamsergrund valley
looking towards
Schlegeis, with the
Olperer just peeking
through the clouds*

Here you have a choice of routes to the Olperer
Hut. If the weather is good follow Route 528 across the
hillside until the route joins with the Neumarkter Runde
Panoramaweg from Schlegeis. If the weather is poor, it is
quicker and more straightforward to take the well-worn
tourist trail back down the valley to Schlegeis, then follow the (short) route to the hut (ZRR Stage 6).

Needless to say, the route description here is for
reversing the latter stages of Stage 2 of the South Tirol
Tour, traversing high across the hillside and shadowing
the Tuxer Hauptkamm ridge.

From the police building, continue down the service road, noted as 'Hochettleck', for around 500 metres
to where the road turns to head down the valley (signpost). Here strike off left, heading N over the open, rocky
ground of Stampler Boden to a footbridge and area where
many streams congregate, some of which are aggres-
sive, until you reach a **footbridge** to cross the noisy
Zamserbach river.

The route now turns more NE to progress across the
well-laid-out rocky path traversing the rocky slopes of

the Lenzen, Wantler and Ebenler, making a rising traverse for 1km until it rounds the foot of the Karstenschneid ridge at **2394m**, where there is a very large man-made *Steinmandl* (stone man) **cairn**.

The route now turns left and traverses around the open amphitheatre-type corrie of the Ober Schrammachkar boulder field on the 2400m contour, crossing two glacial rivers on the way to a second stone **cairn** at the foot of the Ameiskopf spur (**2465m**).

Rounding the ridge, the track comes to a sudden halt after 500 metres, where you will come across a very large signboard stating that the route ahead (to the Geraer Hut) is *Gesprutt* (closed and diverted). ▶ This point is approximately halfway but easier ground lies ahead.

At the signpost you will be directed to descend N on the rocky slope to a series of small ponds at Hinterboden where the trail joins with the Neumarkter Runde Panoramaweg coming up the valley from Schlegeis by Routes 535, 528 and 502, better known as the Central Alpine Way, heading for the demanding high alpine pass of the Alpeiner Scharte to the Geraer Hut. Several signposts point to a footbridge to cross the gorge of the **Unterschrammachbach**. **A little over 3hr**

From here on, the route is quite obvious and follows the **Neumarkter Runde Panoramaweg** to the **Olperer Hut**. **2hr**

See also ZRR Stage 6.

This marks the end of the original route, which changed irrevocably due to a massive rockfall in 2002 that totally obliterated the track between the Geraer Hut and Pfitscherjochhaus.

STAGE 4
Olperer Hut to Friesenberghaus

Start	Olperer Hut (2389m)
Finish	Friesenberghaus (2498m)
Distance	4km
Ascent	200m
Descent	190m
Standard time	2½–3hr
Note	For map, see ZRR, Stage 7

While somewhat short in duration, this very pleasant half-day tour traverses high above the Zamsergrund valley. Be careful when descending the steep rocks to the Friesenbergsee lake, not forgetting to recce the route beforehand to the Friesenbergscharte (2912m), the highest point on the Peter Habeler and Olperer Runde Tour.

This route is shared with, and as described in, the ZRR Stage 7.

See also Excursions from the Friesenberghaus and the tour for the half-day climb of the Hoher Riffler and the shorter tour to Peterskoepfl (ZRR Stage 7).

STAGE 5

Friesenberghaus to Tuxerjochhaus via Friesenbergscharte

Start	Friesenberghaus (2498m)
Finish	Tuxerjochhaus (2316m)
Distance	8.75km
Ascent	620m
Descent	650m
Standard time	6–7hr

The crux of this tour involves crossing the Friesenbergscharte, the highest point of the tour at 2912m, which provides a superb day of mountaineering full of challenge and scenic variety.

This is perhaps the most challenging day of the tour, possibly only surpassed by the Alpeiner Scharte on the Olperer Runde Tour. It is also one of the most scenic days. The scenery throughout is excellent, particularly early in the day when there are fine panoramas of the Hoher Riffler and

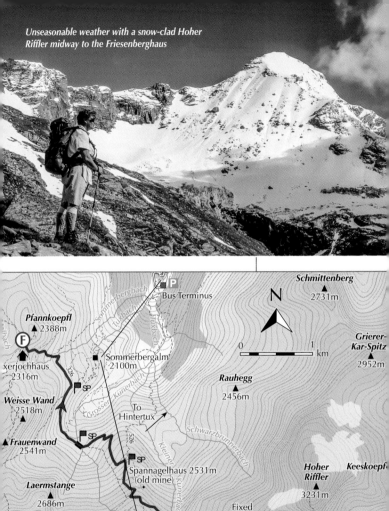

Unseasonable weather with a snow-clad Hoher Riffler midway to the Friesenberghaus

Schmittenberg
2731m

Pfannkoepfl
2388m

Grierer-
Kar-Spitz
2952m

F

xerjochhaus
2316m

N

0   1
km

Bus Terminus

P

Sommerbergalm
2100m

Rauhegg
2456m

Weisse Wand
2518m

To
Hintertux

Frauenwand
2541m

Spannagelhaus 2531m
(old mine)

Hoher
Riffler
3231m

Keeskoepf

Laermstange
2686m

Tuxer Fernerhaus
2660m

Fixed
ropes

FRIESENBERGKAR

Fixed wires
Option 2

Friesenbergscharte
2912m
Gefrorenekees

Peterskoepfl
2679m

Geofrorene-Wand-Kees

Fixed
ropes

Friesenbergsee

Kleiner Kaserer
3093m

Gefrorene-
Wand-Spitzen
3288m

Option 1

Friesenberghaus
2498m

S

Großer
Kaserer
3263m

the immediate scenery across the Friesenbergsee and beyond towards Schlegeis. Once over the Friesenbergscharte, the valley of the Tuxertal and the mountains of Tuxer Alpen entertain.

This is a superb day out with a lot of up and down, perhaps the best day of the Peter Habeler Runde Tour, with excellent scenery throughout.

CAUTIONARY NOTES

The standard time for the route is given as 5hr, but given the distance and terrain involved this is woefully inadequate, with anything between 6 and 7hr being more realistic. The route is also a fine-weather route, as the terrain on the immediate Tuxerjoch side of the Friesenbergscharte and Tux valley is not the easiest, being quite scrappy in places, not helped when route finding is not always obvious.

The final approach to the Friesenbergscharte is very steep and while it is fitted with fixed wires, it is recommended that you use an improvised harness for added security. Similarly, the Friesenbergscharte itself is a very tight col with space for only a few people to pass each other.

From Friesenberghaus you can approach the Friesenbergscharte via two routes.

Option 1: Reverse and return the route from the previous day to the signpost passed en route from the Olperer Hut. This has the advantage of retracing familiar ground and does not involve any technical ground over boulders and patches of snow. **1hr** from the hut to the signpost.

Option 2: Follow the direction of the signpost immediately outside the hut for Peterskoepfl, Hoher Riffler and Friesenbergscharte. Follow the route to the col for the Peterskoepfl. **¾hr** Turn left and cross the **Friesenbergkar** boulder field of large blocks to a signpost and junction of the route heading off to climb the Hoher Riffler. **¼hr** Continue as before over the well-marked boulder field, usually interspersed with patches of snow, to the signpost at the foot of the **Friesenbergscharte**. **¾hr** From here

Difficult ground on the approach to the Friesenbergscharte

there are great views back across the Friesenbergsee to the central peaks of the Zillertal.

Continue and ascend the steep slope ahead, which zigzags to and fro with fixed wires on the steeper, more exposed parts, until just below the Friesenbergscharte when the ground cranks up a few more degrees on the final pull up over rocks to the very tight *Scharte* (col) and signpost. **1hr ▶**

From the *Scharte*, descend rocks, boulders and loose shale to the upper boulder field of the once mighty Gefrorene-Wand-Kees glacier. Follow this over rocks and patches of snow to the signpost at a junction of paths, the left turn-off being for skiers when there is good snow cover. **1–1¼hr** With Spannagelhaus now in sight, continue as before on the uphill track, crossing an obvious glacial stream and eventually arriving at the **Spannagelhaus** (site of an old minerals mine) restaurant

Here a whole new vista opens up to reveal the Hintertux valley and the Tuxerjochhaus sitting on its little col in the far distance.

for well-earned refreshments (no overnight accommodation). **¾hr**

If the weather is poor, and the cable-car system is operative, you can save quite a few hours of descent by making your way to the Tuxer Fernerhaus cable-car station, just 15min away, and taking the cable car to the bottom station at Sommerbergalm to pick up the trail once more to Tuxerjochhaus. Otherwise, descend into the Tux valley, following the service road and making use of the footpath shortcuts across the hairpin bends to a junction of paths with signpost. Route 526 continues to descend to the alpine resort of Hintertux. Continue as before, but now on **Route 326**, over a substantial **footbridge** with signpost thereafter. **1hr** Continue on a good footpath across the hillside to reach the service road for the hut. Either follow the road or path shortcuts to reach the very pleasant **Tuxerjochhaus**. **1hr**

STAGE 6
Tuxerjochhaus to Geraer Hut

Start	Tuxerjochhaus (2316m)
Finish	Geraer Hut (2326m)
Distance	9.25km
Ascent	620m
Descent	750m
Standard time	6–7hr

If blessed with *Kaiser Wetter* (weather fit for a king) this is a superb day out in the mountains, albeit a long one, with quality alpine walking and such excellent views of the Olperer that some say this is the most scenic day of the entire tour.

CAUTIONARY NOTES

While the standard time is given optimistically as 5hr, something between 6–7 hr is more realistic.

Although the route has no real mountaineering challenges similar to those of the Friesenbergscharte, there is the odd place that is very steep, not forgetting all the streams and rivers to be crossed. Needless to say, this is very much a fine-weather route as the terrain between the Kaserer Schartl and the Kleegrubenscharte is not the easiest, being quite scrappy in places, not helped when route finding is not always obvious.

From the hut, with a great view of the Olperer, pick up **Route 527** and follow the excellent path, gradually gaining height until you reach a **small pond**. ½hr Continue as before, climbing steadily on a good path across the ridge of the **Frauenwand** and the junction of paths coming from Hintertux at the **Kaserer Schartl** (2446m) (signpost). **1hr**

Continue around the head of the corrie of Hochgeloate on the 2440m contour, crossing a

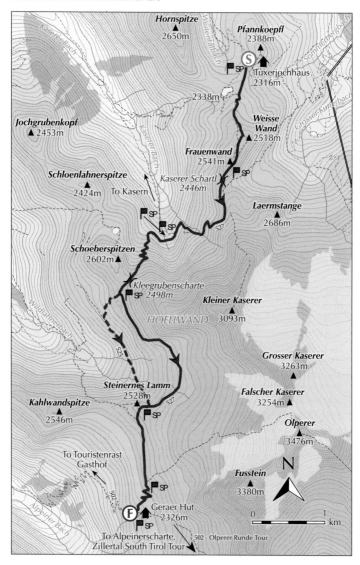

congregation of several streams, with good views down the valley to the tiny village of Kasern.

At the highpoint the route descends steeply down the rib of the Schafleger, where sheep rest and where the track meets the path, signpost, coming up the valley from Kasern. **1hr**

Round the Totegrube (as in nothing grows there) and start to make the steepish ascent of the Kleegrube to the **Kleegrubenscharte** (2498m) (signpost). **1½hr**

Having climbed to this high point, you will be able to see the next high point of Steinernes Lamm (2528m) way across the valley, but it will take quite some time to get there.

From the col, descend first over a rocky trail then high alpine pasture, passing a series of **ponds** to pass the foot of the Nordere Hollwand spur. Ahead lies a series of streams-cum-rivers running down off the Olperer. Cross these with care, and then finally make the rising climb over and around blocks and boulders to the non-descript **Steinernes Lamm** col with its tiny lake at 2528m. **1½hr**

Alternatively, from the Kleegrubenscharte descend for around 150m to a vague track heading of left (SE) and follow this around the mountainside on the 2500m contour to pick up the trail to the Steinernes Lamm. Be careful among the rocks and boulders after crossing the ridge of the Hollwand spur as the path/trail is not well marked and is very problematic in poor weather. ▶ If in doubt, stick to the route described even if you do lose a few hundred metres of height.

Continue now over the much easier ground of the paved paths of the Koattennen bowl to cross the upper reaches of the Wandschaufelgrube gorge and the boulder-strewn river and continue the gradual descent to the **Geraer Hut**. **1hr**

Hopefully, this old route will be given better demarcation with the gaining popularity of the Peter Habeler Runde Tour.

STAGE 7
Geraer Hut to Touristenrast Gasthof

Start	Geraer Hut (2326m)
Finish	Touristenrast Gasthof (1345m)
Distance	7.5km
Ascent	Negligible; all downhill
Descent	980m
Standard time	2½–3hr

The route of this last stage of the tour takes you back down into the valley, passing through the high alp and forest to finish in Touristenrast Gasthof.

Geraer Hut interior

The end of the tour is a simple affair of following the path of the Central Alpine Way, on **Route 502**, back down the

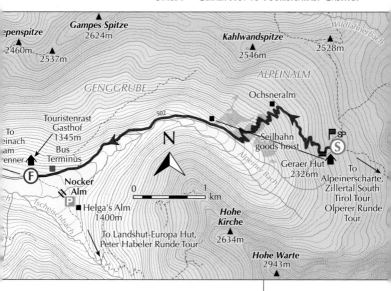

valley through the forest to **Touristenrast Gasthof** and awaiting the Postbus service back to Steinach am Brenner and the train to Innsbruck.

But before doing so, spend an hour exploring the old mine workings, just above the Geraer Hut, which date back to World War 2, when mines formed part of the German Reich's war machine.

See 'Hut directory', 'Geraer Hut'.

TREK 3
Olperer Runde Tour

Start	Touristenrast Gasthof
Finish	Touristenrast Gasthof
Distance	45km
Ascent	3120m
Descent	3270m
Time	6 days
Excursions	Hoher Riffler, Peterskoepfl

While the official leaflet published by the tourist information offices of Mayrhofen, Wipptal and Sterzing states that
the Olperer Runde Tour may be started at any of the main
valley villages or huts, the author's recommendation is
to start and finish the tour at the Touristenrast Gasthof at
the head of the Valsertal valley, undertaking the Olperer
Runde Tour as follows: Touristenrast Gasthof to Olperer
Hut, then Friesenberghaus, Tuxerjochhaus, Geraer Hut
and finishing at Touristenrast Gasthof.

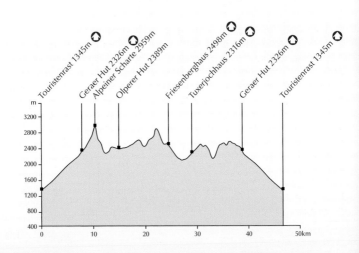

- Stage 1 Touristenrast Gasthof to Geraer Hut 3–4hr
- Stage 2 Geraer Hut to Olperer Hut via Alpeiner Scharte 7–8hr
- Stage 3 Olperer Hut to Friesenberghaus 2½–3hr
- Stage 4 Friesenberghaus to Tuxerjochhaus via Friesenbergscharte 6–7hr
- Stage 5 Tuxerjochhaus to Geraer Hut 6–7hr
- Stage 6 Geraer Hut to Touristenrast Gasthof 2½–3hr

Looking towards the ponds at Hinterboden from below the Alpeiner Scharte

Stage 1: Touristenrast Gasthof to Geraer Hut
8km, 930m ascent, negligible descent, 3–4hr
Follow the Zillertal South Tirol Tour Stage 1 to the Geraer Hut.

Stage 2: Geraer Hut to Olperer Hut via Alpeiner Scharte (2959m)
7.5km, 750m ascent, 700m descent, 7–8hr
Follow the Zillertal South Tirol Tour Stage 2 across the Alpeiner Scharte, descending as far as the alpine tarns/ ponds at Hinterboden. From there follow the Neumarkter Runde Panoramaweg to the Olperer Hut.

Stage 3: Olperer Hut to Friesenberghaus
4km, 200m ascent, 190m descent, 2½–3hr
Follow the Zillertal Rucksack Route Stage 7 and Peter Habeler Runde Tour Stage 4.

Stage 4: Friesenberghaus to Tuxerjochhaus via Friesenbergscharte (2912m)
8.75km, 620m ascent, 650m descent, 6–7hr
Follow the Peter Habeler Runde Tour Stage 5.

Stage 5: Tuxerjochhaus to Geraer Hut
9.25km, 620m ascent, 750m descent, 6–7hr
Follow the Peter Habeler Runde Tour Stage 6.

Stage 6: Geraer Hut to Touristenrast Gasthof
7.5km, negligible ascent, 980m descent, 2½–3hr
Follow the Peter Habeler Runde Tour Stage 7.

Approaching the Geraer Hut

ZILLERTAL
SOUTH TIROL
TOUR

*Descending the Schwarzensteinkees glacier – note safe
distance for glacier travel (Stage 7)*

TREK 4
Zillertal South Tirol Tour

Start	Touristenrast Gasthof
Finish	Mayrhofen
Distance	61km
Ascent	5010m
Descent	4670m
Time	7 days
Excursions	Hochfeiler, Grosser Moeseler, Schwarzenstein

No trip to the Zillertal would be complete without making an excursion to explore the Zillertal peaks of the South Tirol.

The South Tirol refers to the now Italian Sud Tirol, the Alto Adige, a previous Austrian province that was annexed to Italy after World War 1. Apart from the land that was lost, the Deutscher und Osterreichischer

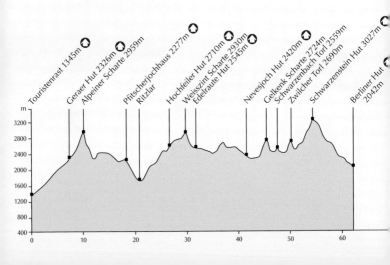

Alpenverein lost a total of 72 huts, all forfeited to Italy as war reparations, including the four huts that will be visited during this short exploratory tour.

This Zillertal South Tirol Tour starts at the approach to the Brenner pass into Italy, at the small town of Steinach am Brenner from where we travel by Postbus to the farming alm at Touristenrast in the Valsertal valley and onto the Geraer Hut. From here the tour enters the Zillertal and South Tirol, heading to the privately owned Pfitscherjochhaus just above Schlegeis at the head of the Zamsergrund valley and Mayrhofen. This is followed by a visit to the Hochfeiler Hut, to climb the Zillertal's highest peak, the Hochfeiler (3510m), the only peak in the Zillertal over 3500m. Thereafter, the route follows the Neveser and Stabebeler Hoehenweg to the historic Edelraut and Nevesjoch Huts from where the Grosser

The Nevesjoch Hut on the Nevesjoch pass

Moeseler is climbed, with an option to descend the mountain across the border into Austria. The final challenge of this tour is the demanding hut-to-hut route to the EU-protected Schwarzenstein Hut before the final part of our journey across the Schwarzensteinkees or Floitenkees glaciers back into Austria.

Throughout the tour you will be constantly reminded of past conflicts: the impact of World Wars 1 and 2 and the difficulty of coming to terms with civil strife when cross-border smuggling and insurgency was rife.

- Stage 1 Touristenrast Gasthof to Geraer Hut 3–4hr
- Stage 2 Geraer Hut to Pfitscherjochhaus 6–7hr
- Stage 3 Pfitscherjochhaus to Hochfeiler Hut 6–7hr
- *Excursion: Ascent of Hochfeiler (3510m) ascent 3hr, descent 2–2½hr*
- Stage 4 Hochfeiler Hut to Edelraut Hut 3hr
- Stage 5 Edelraut Hut to Nevesjoch Hut 3–5hr
- *Excursion: Ascent of Grosser Moeseler (3480m) ascent 4–5hr, descent 3hr*
- Stage 6 Nevesjoch Hut to Schwarzenstein Hut 8–10hr
- Stage 7 Schwarzenstein Hut to Berliner Hut or Greizer Hut 6hr or 3–4hr

Getting to the start

From Innsbruck railway station, take the regional train to Steinach am Brenner, a small town on the Austrian side of the Brenner pass. Trains depart at 09:22/10:22/11:22hr.

Should you have to stay overnight in Steinach, the Hotel Zur Rose is recommended as an alternative start and finish point to Innsbruck; see Appendix A.

From the railway station in Steinach, take the local Postbus service, by the railway station, to Touristenrast Gasthof in the Valsertal valley, a journey just short of one hour. Note there is no bus service on Sunday (if necessary, make use of the local taxi service available) and there is no overnight accommodation at Touristenrast, which is a shame as it would be a great place to stay.

THE SOUTH TIROL, A POTTED HISTORY

As you cross the Pfitscherjoch into Italy and the South Tirol, it's hard to imagine that this whole area just over 100 years ago was a heavily fortified theatre of war.

It all started on the 28 June 1914 when Archduke Franz Ferdinand, heir to the throne of the Austrian Hungarian Empire, along with his wife Sophia, were murdered, by definition assassinated, by Gavrilo Princip, a Bosnian Serb nationalist, while they were on a state visit to the Serbian city of Sarajavo. One month later on 28 July 1914, in retaliation the Austro-Hungarian Empire declared war on Serbia. The Russians went to the aid of Serbia, and Germany entered the fray by declaring war on Russia while simultaneously pressing Italy as a partner of the Triple Alliance of Italy-Austria-Hungary to support Austria, which Italy refused to do in the hope of remaining neutral, as the Triple Alliance was a defensive agreement not an offensive one. France, invaded by Germany, then went to the aid of Russia with the intent of winning back the Alsace-Lorraine region, which they had lost to Prussia (Germany) in the Franco-Prussian War of 1870, when France had tried to reassert its dominant position in Europe. Great Britain being part of the Entente Alliance of Great Britain, France and Russia went to the aid of France when Belgium's sovereignty was invaded, declaring war on Germany on 4 August 1914, all of which led in a few short weeks to the outbreak of the World War 1 in 1914.

Italy, by early 1915, was placed between a rock and a hard place and had great difficulty in remaining neutral during the early stages of the war, particularly with much sabre rattling coming from its historic enemy in the north, and it was more or less forced to join the Entente Alliance or cede more territory to the Austro-Hungarian Empire. Italy eventually decided to ally with the Entente Alliance on 24 May 1915, fighting against the new Triple Alliance of Germany, Austria and Hungary.

Four years later, with most of Europe in ruins, Germany had been defeated and the Austro-Hungarian Empire lay in tatters. The victorious Italians took full control of the South Tirol from the 3 November 1918 onwards when the armistice was proclaimed and marched north into Austria and Innsbruck to take up occupation of the North Tyrol.

At the Treaty of St-Germain on 10 September 1919, instigated by the Entente Alliance powers, in particular the United States, President Woodrow Wilson ignored a plea for clemency and help by all the Mayors of the Sud Tirol, opting to press ahead with the annexation of the whole of the South Tirol to Italy, almost as a collective pique of anger as a penalty for starting the war in the first place and for war repartitions in general. It was a decision made in haste that Wilson is said to have later deeply regretted. The annexation included the forfeit of 72 mountain huts that belonged to the Deutscher und Osterreichischer Alpenverein, including four huts that are visited during this short tour.

Formal annexation took place on 10 October 1920 and affected 150,000 people, a decision that would have a profound effect on the South Tirol region for the next 50 years.

During the 1920s and 1930s, Austria was a broken and bankrupt country and this led to much cross-border smuggling and insurgency. During the open-door policy of Anschluss with Germany in March 1938, Austria became an extended province of Germany; again, the hope was that the South Tirol would be returned to the (Austria) Third Reich and German-speaking peoples. That hope was dashed when Germany became allied to Mussolini's fascist Italy. In 1939, the dictator Mussolini decreed that all of the indigenous German-speaking people of the South Tirol should become Italianised or should leave Italy and the South Tirol for good and emigrate to the new lands of the Third Reich and Greater Germany. Of those who did leave, some had little choice, including the *Huettenwirtin* at the Edelraut Hut. Most went to German-annexed western Poland where after the war they were persecuted as Nazi sympathisers; similarly, those who stayed in the South Tirol were persecuted by the Italians.

After the surrender of Italy in 1943, the South Tirol was occupied by the German Army, including all the huts along the border of the South Tirol, until the eventual German retreat and surrender of Austria in 1945.

By 1948 most of the huts had been returned to their rightful owners, but many were in a derelict state and those that weren't were occupied by the Italian military.

Once again, the South Tirol political question raised its head with Austria asking for its return. Counter insurgency across the border and the smuggling of goods once again became rife. All the huts along the South Tirol became garrisoned by the Italian Army and when they did eventually vacate in the late 1960s and 1970s, most huts were in ruins or had been blown up.

By 1972 the South Tirol was decreed a bilingual, semi-autonomous state of Italy. However, the ties with Austria strengthened when Austria joined the European Union in 1995 and the border controls with Italy disappeared, particularly across the Brenner pass; this went someway to reuniting Austria with its beloved South Tirol.

Finally, despite all this conflict – the spilt blood of two World Wars – the South Tirol is the most productive and wealthiest state in Italy and it is also a brilliant place to go mountaineering.

STAGE 1

Touristenrast Gasthof to Geraer Hut

Start	Touristenrast Gasthof (1345m)
Finish	Geraer Hut (2326m)
Distance	8km
Ascent	800m
Descent	Negligible
Standard time	3–4hr
Note	For map, see PHRT Stage 7. See 'Getting to the start' for information about getting to Touristenrast. There is no overnight accommodation at Touristenrast

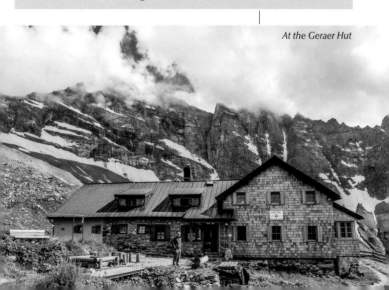

At the Geraer Hut

From the Touristenrast guest house, continue up the Valsertal valley to the end of the service track road to the *Seilbahn* (goods hoist lift) (signpost). **¾hr**

Here on, follow the obvious trail NE on a good path through the forest for a short 2hr to farm buildings and an alm at Ochsner Hut (2081m), on the grassy slopes of Alpeinalm. **2hr** Once into open landscape, the trail climbs steadily, heading SE, eventually crossing two footbridges and the small gorge of Windschaufelgraben with a river, not too distant from the **Geraer Hut**. **1hr**

STAGE 2
Geraer Hut to Pfitscherjochhaus

Start	Geraer Hut (2326m)
Finish	Pfitscherjochhaus (2275m)
Distance	10.25km
Ascent	About 1300m
Descent	970m
Standard time	6–7hr

On a fine, sunny day this high-mountain tour is in the top drawer of alpine promenades, encompassing challenges – crossing one of the few weaknesses in the main Tuxer Hauptkamm ridge – good scenery and a little history for good measure.

On leaving the hut, you cannot but notice how stark the scenery is with the wall-to-wall mountains of Schrammacher and Fusstein and hardly a blade of grass anywhere. Within a short time, your attention will be drawn to the old mine workings built during World War 2. The mining pylons and support building have largely disappeared into history, and the entrance to the mine remains soundly bolted and strictly *Verboten* (forbidden).

Crossing the Alpeiner Scharte on a good day, you will find the views limited to the west, towards the Stubai Alps, and the ground immediately ahead, which steepens considerably to provide some excitement on fixed wires. Beyond the *Scharte*, the whole route opens up, but the high peaks

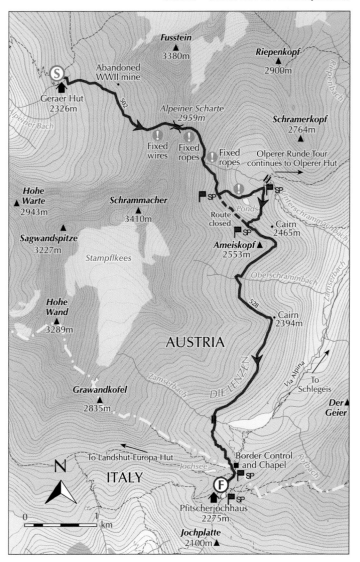

Fusstein
3380m

Riepenkopf
2900m

S
Geraer Hut
2326m

Abandoned
WWII mine

Alpeiner Scharte
2959m

Schramerkopf
2764m

Alpeiner Bach

502

Fixed wires   Fixed ropes   Fixed ropes

Olperer Runde Tour
continues to Olperer Hut

SP

Hohe
Warte
2943m

Schrammacher
3410m

Unterschrammachbach

SP

Ponds

Route
closed

Cairn
2465m

Sagwandspitze
3227m

Stampflkees

Ameiskopf
2553m

Oberschrammbach

Hohe
Wand
3289m

528

Zamserbach

Cairn
2394m

AUSTRIA

Zamserbach

DIE LENZEN

Via Alpina

To
Schlegeis

Grawandkofel
2835m

Der
Geier

N

0   1
         km

To Landshut-Europa Hut

Jochsee

Border Control
and Chapel

SP

ITALY

F
Pfitscherjochhaus
2275m

SP

Rotbach

Jochplatte
2100m

167

are barred from view by many ridges in all directions. The route descends equally as steeply on the east side as it does to the west before easing into a very pleasant alpine trail until you are stopped in your tracks by the rock avalanche that obliterated the trail in 2002. Sadly, there are no nice words to describe getting across this stone-swept couloir which now requires a one-hour detour to negotiate what was a few hundred metres of open ground. Hopefully the track will be restored in the near future. Thereafter, the next few hours to the hut are an absolute pleasure of an alpine walk, with a painstakingly laid-out path and fine views down towards Schlegeis and the Zillertal valley.

CAUTIONARY NOTES

This route, in the main, is a fine-weather route. If it's raining at the Geraer Hut, it will definitely be sleeting, if not snowing, at the *Scharte*, which is just short of 3000m. The top of the Alpeiner Scharte on both sides of the col is exceedingly steep and despite the availability of fixed wires, it is not a place to be practising snow skills. Thereafter, the route diversion down into the glacial basin of Hinterboden is not at present a frequented trail and the area is very problematic in mist and rain when route finding is not that obvious. Further ahead, crossing the numerous streams at Die Lenzen is not without drama, particularly if the streams are in flood, as these streams are more raging torrent than babbling brook; if you are in a group, stay close together for support.

Alternative Start from Mayrhofen
For participants starting from Mayrhofen, take the local bus service to Schlegeis (see 'Local transport' in 'Introduction'), then follow the route description noted as the alternative route to the Olperer Hut for Stage 7 of the ZRR.

Main route
From the hut (signpost) follow **Route 502** on the Central Alpine Way from which, provided it is a clear day, the Alpeiner Scharte is clearly visible to the east. The path of sorts progresses across broken, rocky ground where after an hour or so remnants of mining activity come into

view: ruins of old buildings, steel structures and pylons used during World War 2 to mine chrome molybdenum, used for making chrome steel. **1hr** From here on, the path gets steeper and less obvious. Continue as before over open rocky slopes, now with more slabs and boulders, zigzagging to and fro. Just below the **Alpeiner Scharte** (2959m) the path steepens considerably, with fixed wires in place, to the col (signpost). **1hr**

From the col, descend the very steep, rocky slope first E then SE over difficult ground of shale and loose rock until the slope gradually eases at a huge *Steinmandl* (stone cairn). ▶

There are excellent views towards Schlegeis but sadly all the main peaks remain hidden.

Continue S over open rocky ground, descending gradually for about 1km until the path becomes blocked and peters out at a gulley and old glacial moraine. **1hr** Here the track was washed out by a landslide in 2002, forcing the route to be diverted east into the large open corrie of Schrammachkar to pick up the trail to the Olperer Hut; this diversion, until the trail is restored, will add at least 1hr to what was previously 500 metres of open ground. Descend NE over difficult, broken ground, following the left bank of the stream and attendant moraine, heading for the large open marshy area of Hinterboden, complete with a number of small alpine tarns and ponds. After around 100m of descent, cross the moraine and stream E, heading across open country to pick up the trail of Route 502 coming from the Olperer Hut. **1½hr** There signposts hereabouts but they are not obvious, particularly in mist. Thereafter, reascend the rocky slope SW to reconnect with the original path to complete the detour. ▶ **1hr**

On this side of the detour is a very large signboard stating that the route ahead is Gesprutt (closed).

Back on the trail proper, but now on **Route 528**, head SE on a very good rocky path to a large *Steinmandl* (**stone cairn**) at the foot of the spur on the Ameiskopf ridge. Round the foot of the ridge and traverse around the open amphitheatre-type corrie of the Oberschrammachkar boulder field, heading for a second large stone cairn 1km away, crossing two glacial rivers on the way. Here there are excellent views towards Schlegeis and the Zillertal valley.

Continue as before (SW) on an excellent rocky path that has been painstakingly laid out, partly paved in places, traversing the rocky slopes of Die Ebenler and Die Wantler until you reach the head water of the Zamserbach stream and river; fortunately, this noisy, raging water is crossed by a **footbridge**. **1hr**

◀ The track of sorts heads S over open rocky ground interspersed with streams and marshy ground to eventually join the broad track coming up the valley from Schlegeis and Mayrhofen. After a short stroll you will emerge on the border with the South Tirol at the *Zollwachhuette*, the old **border control and customs police hut**. After a further 300 metres along the now graded single-track road you will reach the **Pfitscherjochhaus**. **1hr**

STAGE 3
Pfitscherjochhaus to Hochfeiler Hut

Start	Pfitscherjochhaus (2275m)
Finish	Hochfeiler Hut (2710m)
Distance	9km
Ascent	900m
Descent	530m
Standard time	6–7hr

This is a particularly fine walk, with an excellent variety of alpine scenery, crosses one of the few weaknesses in the main Tuxer Hauptkamm ridge.

The initial stages are dominated by a particularly fine chocolate-box scene down the Pfitscher Tal valley to St Jakob. Sadly, this vista is all but lost on entering the forest and woodland area until the mountains reveal themselves once more when the Hochfeiler Hut comes into view. From here on, you are in fine alpine territory with an open rocky terrain of spiky pinnacles and some of the finest glaciated and snow-covered peaks in the Zillertal.

Those interested in alpine history should spend some time searching out the location of the old hut and maybe ponder where the Victorian artist ET Compton pitched his canvas and easel when he painted his scene of the Wiener Hut in 1900. The painting was gifted to the Austrian Alpine Club in 1966 and now hangs proudly in the Alpenverein Museum in Innsbruck.

CAUTIONARY NOTES

This is a particularly straightforward, pleasant day's outing with little to hinder one's progress. However, take care rounding the crags above Platte Glidergang and crossing the difficult boulder ground at Weisskar. While there are a number of footbridges in place, they have been known, at times, to not survive the winter.

From the hut, head S along the hut's service road. After around 100 metres you will come to some **old army**

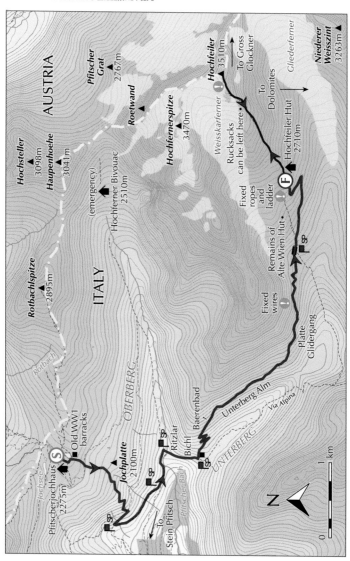

barracks; first occupied by the Austrians prior to World War 1, they were later used by the Italian military up to the early 1960s. Continue down the road until you come to a signpost indicating the first of the shortcuts across the service road. Head SW across the gentle, open grassy slopes of the Via Alpina trail. ▶ The path descends gradually over open ground at first then, after around 1km, continues more steeply when it enters woodland to join the service road once more. The service road turns SE and after a further 1km comes to a car park and picnic area noted as **Ritzlar** (signpost). **1½hr** The signpost declares that the Hochfeiler Hut is some 3hr and 10min distant when in reality it is a minimum of 4hr.

The observant will be able to pick out an old army trench system, albeit overgrown, from an era fortunately long past.

Head S following a good path through the quiet of the forest to a group of farm-type woodland buildings at **Bichl** (signpost). The path now pitches up a few degrees and starts to climb, zigzagging E across vegetated slopes, gradually emerging onto more open ground on the 2000m contour at **Baerenbad**. **1½hr**

The track, now more of a rocky path than vegetated trail, continues to climb steadily for another hour across the open slopes of the Unterbergalm, coming to a natural

Crossing one of the many streams, with the Hochfeiler Hut in the far distance

This is a good place for a break, with fine views towards the glaciated peaks and Hoher Weisszint.

conclusion at **Platte Glidergang**. As you round the rocky buttress of Blauer Kofel, the Hochfeiler Hut comes into view some 500m higher and still over 2km away. ◄ **1hr**

The character of the route now changes, becoming more mountainous. Climb the rocky slopes ahead and traverse E under the crags of Schoassen, crossing a number of gullies with **fixed wires** in place before descending towards the foot of the terminal moraine of the **Weisskarferner glacier**, where many streams congregate. Cross over the streams, making use of the footbridges, to the start of the zigzags leading to the hut (signpost). **1hr** If you take the left-hand track, you will come to the site of the original Wiener Hut, which was blown up in 1962 by the Italian Army as a deterrent to would-be South Tirol insurgents and would-be smugglers. However, the main track is the one to the right, which climbs the gravel path more gradually to the very robust **Hochfeiler Hut. 1hr**

EXCURSION

Ascent of Hochfeiler (3510m)

Start	Hochfeiler Hut (2710m)
Distance	4km
Ascent	800m
Grade	F+
Standard time	Ascent 3–4hr; descent about 2–2½hr
Note	For map, see Stage 3

This is a justifiably popular climb on the Zillertal's highest peak, first climbed in 1865 by Paul Grohmann with guides Peter Fuchs and Josele Samer, and it is the only peak in the Zillertal over 3500m.

The route is characterised by excellent scrambling along the south-west ridge, finishing with a climb along an airy snow arête to the summit. Unlike the northern approach from Furtschaglhaus, which is way beyond the scope of the author and these notes and which falls into the domain of serious alpinism, this route from the south has no serious glacial obstacles, putting the route within the capabilities of the most modest of mountaineers.

From the south the climb is very straightforward, with only the last 500m of height requiring modest alpine skills. The views from the summit are extensive, but if you take care and walk along the ridge beyond the summit, they are exceptional: everything is draped in snow, particularly the Hochfeiler's north face and the Grosser Moeseler and the Schwarzenstein across the void. Beyond, all the major peaks are easy to pick out, such as the Olperer, the Oetztal Wildspitze, the Grossglockner and the Dolomites, with the Marmolada to the south.

CAUTIONARY NOTES

For the highest peak in the Zillertal the difficulties are minimal. However, the climb is a fine-weather route. During unsettled weather, the route is best avoided as the ridge and snow arête leading to the summit attract fierce winds that will bowl you over.

Route cairn pointing to the summit

From the hut (signpost) head N, climbing a buttress aided with wire ropes, metal staples and gangway planks to the junction of the alternative path coming up from the site of the Old Wiener Hut (signpost). **½hr**

Turn right (NE) and follow the well-defined ridge, climbing steadily over rock, slabs and boulders. Once you reach point 3119m, the route opens up, with the profile of the final ridge and snow arête leading to the summit of the Hochfeiler, with attendant cross, looking particularly fine.

The scenery is exceptional, as the panorama now includes the Hochfeiler's neighbouring peaks of the Hochferner Spitze and Hoher Weisszint.

Continue to climb over rocks, patches of snow and general broken ground, heading for an obvious dip and col on the ridge. **2½hr** This is a good place for a break and to tackle up with rope, ice axe and crampons, particularly if the ridge is snow covered and corniced. ◄

Continue now in the obvious direction of the ridge and summit beyond. Climb and scramble along the ridge, keeping N on the least exposed side until the rocks meet the snow. From here on, climb the short snow arête to the summit of the **Hochfeiler** (3510m) and its large metal cross. **½hr** Brilliant views stretch to infinity in all directions. Sharp eyes will be able to locate the Furtschaglhaus, just 3km away and 1200m lower to the north.

Return by the same route, taking care while descending the summit ridge until you reach easier ground. **About 2–2½hr**

STAGE 4
Hochfeiler Hut to Edelraut Hut

Start	Hochfeiler Hut (2710m)
Finish	Edelraut Hut (2545m)
Distance	4km
Ascent	250m
Descent	430m
Standard time	3hr

This is a very pleasant walk from the Hochfeiler Hut to one of the most traditional huts in the South Tirol, the Edelraut Hut, also known as the Eisbruggjoch Hut or the Rifugio Passo Ponte di Ghiaccio. Much of this route can be seen and recced from the terrace of the Hochfeiler Hut.

The route offers some excellent scenery, particularly of the previous day's climb up the Hochfeiler, when the whole of the route can be seen in profile. However, the views from the little col at Untere Weisszintscharte are particularly interesting as the land is placed in clear geographic context. Sitting at the col looking west, you will see the peaks of the Stubai Alps and should you have binoculars with you, you should be able to locate the Becherhaus perched on its tiny rocky knoll just to the left of the Wilder Freiger. As you look to the east towards the hut, the jagged peaks of the Dolomites break the horizon like a row of saw teeth. The snowy mantel of the Marmolada stands clear, and the long plateau of Sieser Alm is easy to locate, as are the individual massifs of Rosengarten and Zwoelferkofel.

CAUTIONARY NOTES

The sign outside the Hochfeiler Hut informs you that the Edelraut Hut is a mere 1½hr away. Don't you believe it. This amount of time will only get you as far Untere Weisszintscharte. The short route has few natural hindrances, but take care getting down the moraine onto the glacier, as it is just loose rubble and not very stable under foot. Getting off the glacier and climbing the rock buttress requires using the ladder – if you can reach the rungs; otherwise, you may have to ask your companion for a foot-up. This type of scenario is going to become more common as the glaciers recede and the aid gets further out of reach.

From the hut, head E up the rocky boulder slopes that overlook the **Gliederferner glacier** that gradually descends tottering blocks of rock to the glacier at a little over the 2800m contour (signpost). **¾hr** Get onto the glacier; there's no need to tackle up unless there is snow cover as the glacier is pretty flat and covered in grit, negating the need for crampons. Walk S across the glacier for ½km, heading for a large rock buttress. ▶

Climb the buttress, making use of the staples, ladder rungs and fixed wires, where there are some stiff pull-ups

Look out for excellent views towards the Hochfeiler and Hoher Weisszint.

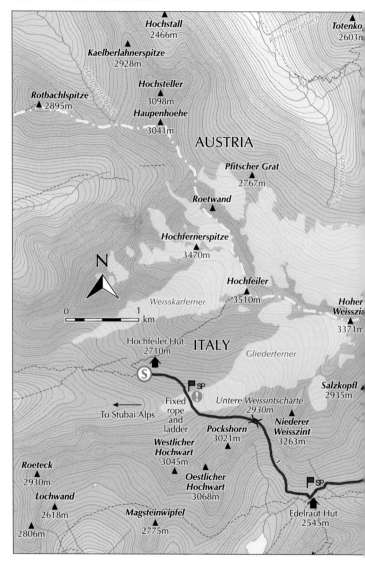

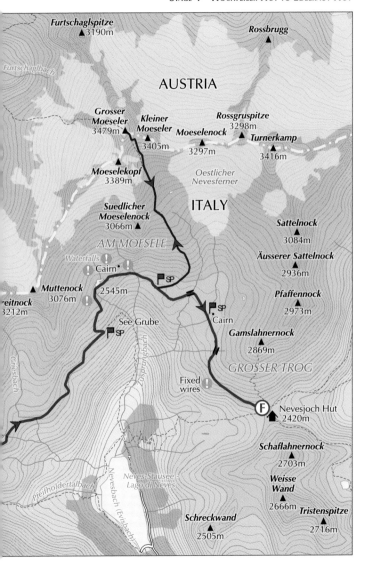

On the Gliederferner glacier

until the ground gradually eases. For those of you who cannot reach the first rung of the ladder, descend the side of the buttress and round its base to a snow gully that can be climbed just as easily as the aid-assisted route. From the top of the buttress the route traverses across more open ground, over patches of snow and rocks, again with fixed wires in places, to finally emerge on the little col of **Untere Weisszintscharte (2930m)** (signpost). **2hr** There are excellent views from the col, and the Edelraut Hut is clearly visible.

For those who had difficulty in getting a mobile phone signal at the Hochfeiler Hut, this little col has excellent mobile phone signals, including international calls if need be!

From the *Scharte* descend SE through a trail of large boulders, some equipped with fixed wires on the exposed sections, until the path gradually eases into a fine rocky paved trail to the very pleasant **Edelraut Hut (2545m)**, perhaps better known on this side of the border by its Italian name Rifugio Passo Ponte di Ghiaccio or the Eisbruggjoch, named after the broad saddle on which it sits.

STAGE 5
Edelraut Hut to Nevesjoch Hut

Start	Edelraut Hut (2545m)
Finish	Nevesjoch Hut (2420m)
Distance	9km
Ascent	About 200m
Descent	About 100m
Standard time	3hr if footbridge is intact; otherwise 5hr
Note	For map, see Stage 4

This is a very pleasant route to the Nevesjoch Hut, also known as the Rifugio Giovanni Porro or the Alte Chemnitzer Hut, although some would say it is a little short in duration.

The route overall is very pleasant with some good alpine walking, particularly the early and latter parts of the journey over painstakingly laid-out paved rocky paths. The scenery is good but not exceptional as the high peaks are very much guarded. However, this is also one of those hut-to-hut connections that has a rather large sting in its tail in the form a ravine midway between the huts. If the footbridge is washed out proceed with the utmost care.

CAUTIONARY NOTES

What should be a very pleasant walk of a few hours could turn into something far more serious when you reach the ravine. Provided the footbridge is in place you will have little to hinder your journey; however, if the bridge has been washed away, you will be seriously challenged. In this case, retrace your steps to the top of the zigzags and head N over open rocky ground where after 150m of uphill you can turn E and make your own way, by Hobson's choice, to cross the glacial melt waters higher up. Once across the stream, more waterfall than babbling brook, scramble down the left bank of the cascading river to pick up the path once more. This diversion will cost you at least 1hr.

Your alternative is to descend the top edge overlooking the right bank of the ravine for around 100m until it's possible to descend into the gully, cross the river and reascend the moraine-type slope on the opposite bank. If on leaving the Edelraut Hut, you have been advised by the *Huettenwirt* that the route is *Gesprutt* (closed), take the vague path as mentioned just beyond Seegrube and cross open ground to pick up the trail beyond but note this traverse is also problematic.

Look back for good views towards the Edelraut Hut.

As you leave behind the very pleasant Edelraut Hut, the Nevesjoch Hut is clearly seen across the valley to the east, some 6km away as the crow flies. Our journey on foot will take us a little further. Head NE along the **Neveser Hoehenweg** on an excellent, paved, rocky track of delightful alpine walking. ◀ Continue as before, following the rocky trail with the Nevesjoch Hut in clear view ahead. After 1hr you will come to a signpost of sorts, namely various directions painted on a large boulder at Seegrube, which points the way down the valley. **1hr**

Round the corner of the rocky rib and climb gradually up to the 2500m contour, where after another short distance you will come to a vague track heading off more N. The main hut-to-hut connecting route is the obvious trail ahead; however – this is why you need to talk to the *Huettenwirt* at the Edelraut before setting out – if the trail ahead is clear and not barred with a pile of rocks, as in *Gesprutt*, then continue as before. If the trail ahead is closed, then either take your chances or follow the vague trail heading off left to the N.

Taking your chances, following the main path, continue as before and after about 1hr you will come to the head of some zigzags that descend to a washed-out ravine complete with **waterfall** (shown on the AV map in tiny blue print as 'wf' for waterfall), which culminates in a menacing noisy river. Cross this 50-metre-wide gap by whatever means, then continue over straightforward rocky ground albeit for a short distance as once more the trail disappears at the edge of another collapsed moraine that has also been washed out, although not as seriously

as the previous one. Descend the moraine of loose rocks and boulders, glued together with mud and grit, and ascend the opposite awkward slope of shale and rubble to get back on the path proper and the open level ground of the **Am Moesele glacial basin**, marked by a large stone cairn. ▶ Round this to a junction of paths that points the way to the Grosser Moeseler (signpost). **1hr**

From here on, continue over open rocky ground. At its lowest point at Grosser Trog the route crosses a simple tree-trunk footbridge complete with another large stone cairn and an elaborate signpost pointing out the directions of the climbs for Turnerkamp and the Grosser Moeseler.

The route continues on much gentler terrain, following an excellent paved path with **fixed wires** on the more exposed sections. After you have rounded the ubiquitous corner, the Edelraut Hut comes back into view as the path descends to the **Nevesjoch Hut**, named after the col on which it sits. **1hr**

This massive stone-swept, amphitheatre-type corrie of huge proportions was left behind by retreating glaciers.

EXCURSION

Ascent of Grosser Moeseler (3480m)

Start	Nevesjoch Hut (2420m)
Distance	11km (about 9km if descending to the Furtschaglhaus)
Ascent	1100m
Grade	PD+
Standard time	Ascent 4–5hr; descent to the Nevesjoch Hut about 3hr; descent to the Furtschaglhaus about 3hr
Note	For map, see Stage 4

This popular route on the Zillertal's third-highest peak is distinctly different to the route from the north. From the south the route is much more straightforward, putting the mountain within the grasp of the most modest of mountaineers.

CAUTIONARY NOTES

The initial part of the route is quite straightforward for aspiring mountaineers, being little more than a stroll over broken ground. However, the last 400 metres of the summit is very steep and exposed when moving together over difficult broken ground.

Needless to say, this is not a route to undertake in less-than-ideal weather.

From the hut retrace your steps along the route to the Edelraut Hut, heading NW along the **Naveser Hoehenweg**. Follow the excellent path first to Grosser Trog, marked with the huge stone cairn and novel signpost that indicates the route to the mountain, then onwards across open ground to the tree-trunk footbridge. An easy walk over open ground follows across the lower slopes of the **Am Moesele** boulder field (signpost). **1–1¼hr**

From here turn right and head N over open rocky ground comprising mostly glacial debris. The route climbs the ridge immediately ahead in a gradual fashion for 1km before the ridge ramps up steeply a few more degrees and becomes more obstructive. Climb through the rock barrier, fixed ropes in place, until the ground gradually eases on the 3000m contour. ▶ With the summit cross in clear view, climb the rocky rib, scrambling here and there over rocks and patches of snow, then veering more NW, heading for an obvious small gap in the Moesele's east ridge. **2hr** Climb the steepening slope, now more snow than rock, to its obvious conclusion, where on arrival you will simply say 'WOW!', as the scenery you're presented with is stunning: a whole mountain landscape of snow and white drapery, with wall-to-wall mountains.

This is a good place to tackle up.

From here on, scramble cautiously along the east ridge for the last 100m of vertical height, very exposed in places, amid alpine scenery that is visually at its best, to reach the summit cross on **Grosser Moeseler (3479m)** and the crossroads with the route from the north and Furtschaglhaus. **1hr**

The summit **views** can be described with words such as 'stunning', 'exceptional', 'brilliant' or

The final summit ridge

simply 'Wow!'. But it is the view on the north side of the mountain that will hold your gaze, particularly along the east ridge towards the Turnerkamp. Turn to the SW to the magnificent ice wall and jumbled maze of crevasses on the Hochfeiler and Hochferner. To the north-west, those with sharp eyes will quickly locate the Furtschaglhaus then the Schlegeis reservoir with the Olperer and Schneegupf snow arête beyond. To the south lies the fertile South Tirol with the Rieserferner Group and further still the unique Dolomites, whose jagged peaks break the horizon like a row of teeth on a saw – simply stunning. Enjoy!

In descent you have a choice. You can reverse the entire route back to the Nevesjoch Hut, taking additional care when descending the first 200m of vertical height after which the ground gets easier. **About 3hr** Alternatively, descend the mountain to the Furtschaglhaus by reversing the route description given when climbing the mountain from the north. **About 3hr** (See ZRR, Stage 5, Excursion: 'Ascent of the Grosser Moeseler'.)

Apart from the odd difficulty, which can be expected on a climb on such a big mountain, the route from the south is totally different in character to that of its counterpart from the north, which is much more difficult.

STAGE 6
Nevesjoch Hut to
Schwarzenstein Hut

Start	Nevesjoch Hut (2420m)
Finish	Schwarzenstein Hut (3027m)
Distance	12km
Ascent	About 1350m
Descent	About 1060m
Standard time	8–10hr

This is a very long-distance stage – and one not to be underestimated – from the Nevesjoch Hut to the Schwarzenstein Hut, also known as Rifugio Vittorio Veneto al Sasso Nero. The route is characterised by the rounding of three huge mountain corrie amphitheatres and the crossing of three very distinctly different cols of *Schartes* and *Torls*. It is a long-distance trail with lots of ups and downs across challenging terrain – and it will really test your stamina. Be on your way early!

This is a true long-distance alpine walk with a sting in its trail, that for those of you who enjoy such challenges you will be in your element.

The route traverses up and down roughly on the 2500m contour high above the Ahrntal valley, and if you are blessed with good weather and blue skies, there is excellent scenery throughout. In mountaineering terms, since the route is almost entirely on rock and crosses a great deal of difficult broken ground, it rates as being at the top end of alpine walking and places a constant demand on basic mountain skills from start to finish.

CAUTIONARY NOTES

Before you set out, make sure you have reserved your bed space at the Schwarzenstein Hut. It would be poor form to have walked for 10 hours to discover there are no beds, only *Notlager* (sleeping with the furniture).

As well as the physical demands of this stage, the route is very remote. The weather is also a major concern since there is nowhere along the entire route to shelter should you need too. Needless to say, you need to be confident about your fitness and the weather.

Most of the route involves crossing numerous boulder fields: some are typical mountain terrain while others pose more of a risk with ankle-twisting, leg-snapping terrain through boulders of car- and house-sized proportions.

From the hut the way ahead is barred by a great wall of mountains that will have to be taken in one's stride. Head E, along the **Stabeler Hoehenweg** on **Route 24A**, which provides easy walking on a good path. After about 1km you will reach a signpost of sorts, namely route directions painted on a large boulder, and a junction with the path coming up the valley from the small village of Luttach. Here the route turns NE, heading into the upper alp, with

AUSTRIA

Am Horn
2647m

Map continues
on page 190

Steinmandl
2634m

**III. Hornspitze
(Berliner Spitze)**
3254m

Rossbrugg

**IV.
Hornspitze**
3085m

I. Hornspitze
3172m

AUSTRIA

Vordere Hornspitze
3148m

Breiter Kopf
2880m

Rossgruspitze
3298m

Turnerkamp
3416m

Schwarzenbach Toerl
2559m

SANDRAIN

oeselenock
3297m

Innere Gruene Plate

*Oestlicher
Nevesferner*

**Aeussere
Gruene Plate**
2800m

Scharhagger
2649m

ITALY

Gelenkscharte
2724m

Gelenknock
2882m

To
Weissenbach

Sattelnock
3084m

. Cairn

Moeselnock
2712m

Aeusserer Sattelnock
2936m

Pfaffennock
2973m

N

Gamslahnernock
2869m

0   1
km

24A Stabeler Hoehenweg

SP

SP

(S) **Nevesjoch Hut**
2420m

Schaflahnernock

2703m

**Weisse
Wand**
2666m **Tristenspitze**
2716m

Schreckwand

the marshy grazing meadows of Inn Goegen Alm. Enjoy the pastoral alpine scenery as you walk towards a foot-bridge and signpost. **1hr**

Cross the **footbridge** and ascend NE across the slopes ahead, climbing through an obvious rock buttress; the *Scharte* is easily seen to the left. As the route levels out, head through, over and around various boulder fields with the usual meandering false trails. The route, marked in places with large purpose-built stone cairns, eventually emerges on the first of the three passes you will cross, the **Gelenkscharte (2724m)** (signpost). **1½hr ▶**

All around there is good, rugged mountain scenery.

From the col, descend NE down difficult, steep, ankle-twisting rocky slopes, with boulders of car- and house-sized proportions, until the ground gradually

Descending difficult, steep ground at the Schwarzenbach Toerl

189

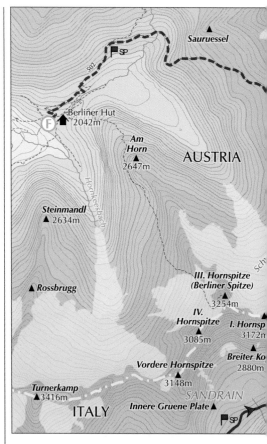

eases below the peaks of the Berliner Spitze to the north and the vast boulder slopes of the Sandrain (on the 2460m contour), created from the retreating Mitterbachkees glacier. A signpost here indicates the route down the valley to Weissenbach. Continue to round the head of the couloir and corrie, ascending steep rocky slopes over difficult broken ground, with fixed wires here and there, to the second of the three

passes, the **Schawarzenbach Toerl (2559m)**, the very aptly named 'Black Gate'. **2hr**

From the Toerl, the route dictates how and where you will descend, giving you no choice but to descend the steep gully ahead, which is near vertical in places. Descend the gully cautiously, making use of the substantial fixed ropes until the ground gradually eases. ▶ At the base of the Toerl, continue NE on the Stabeler

There are good views towards the Schwarzenstein.

Hoehensteig and Route 24A – note the change of name from Hoehenweg to Hoehensteig, the route going from a high-level way to a high-level climb – which due to the nature of the ground is perhaps a better description. The trail continues over wearisome, rocky, broken ground, which has now become a familiar trait and characteristic of this stage. Midway the track is broken by a vague track coming up from the south, from Luttach (signpost). Meanwhile, ahead is the highest and third of the passes you will cross, the **Zwilcher Toerl (2690m)**. Continue as before to round the head of the corrie and couloir, climbing gradually, then much more steeply, on a tight zigzagging rocky trail, with fixed wires in places, to the tight and very enclosed Toerl-cum-gateway, complete with park-bench-type seat and signpost. **2hr** ◄

Unfortunately, over the next section much height is lost. Oh, to be an Adler eagle and cross this great open void in a matter of minutes. From the Toerl descend the steep, rocky slopes of Zu Torla until the ground gradually eases on the 2500m contour. Continue NE over what is now easy ground, rounding the now familiar corrie-type scenery past a small glacial pond and eventual link-up with the path coming up from the valley and Luttach (**signpost**). **2hr**

Having lost so much height in the descent from the Zwilcher Toerl, you are now faced with the sting in the tail: the hut is perched many metres above your head!

The route turns N and after a few hundred metres you will reach a signpost at Ofenleit indicating the way to the Schwarzenstein Hut and across the Trippachschneide ridge to Kegelgasslalm. Keep left (N) and continue to climb the steepening rocky slopes. After another short distance you will reach a second signpost that indicates the *Klettersteig*, the climbing path to the hut. Unless you are blessed with an abundance of energy, it's probably best to stay with the standard route. Continue as before, plodding through a glacial basin of huge boulders, left behind by the retreating glacier, until it is possible to ascend a large patch of permanent snow. Climb this to its head and make an awkward exit onto the rocks on the

Excellent views extend towards the Schwarzenstein, where sharp eyes will be able to locate the hut.

right where there is a vague trail of sorts. Get onto the rocks and traverse the slope in a series of rocky ramps, aided by fixed ropes and ladder-type staples, until the ridge runs out of mountain and you eventually reach the famous **Schwarzenstein Hut**. 1hr

The old Schwarzenstein Hut

STAGE 7

Schwarzenstein Hut to Berliner Hut or Greizer Hut

Start	Schwarzenstein Hut (3027m)
Finish	Berliner Hut (2042m) or Greizer Hut (2226m)
Distance	Berliner Hut 8.75km; Greizer Hut 5.25km
Ascent	To Berliner Hut via the Felskoepfl (3235m) and Schwarzenstein Sattel (3143m) 210m; to Greizer Hut via the Trippachsattel (3028m) negligible
Descent	To the Berliner Hut via the Schwarzenstein Sattel 880m; to the Greizer Hut via the Trippachsattel 700m
Standard time	Berliner Hut 6hr; Greizer Hut 3–4hr
Note	For map, see Stage 6

A choice of routes back to Austria presents itself, both of which are of equal merit.

For those of you who made the effort to undertake Stage 4 of the ZRR, traversing the Schwarzenstein from the Greizer Hut to the Berliner Hut, you will have come full circle. For those who opted for the normal route between the Greizer Hut and the Berliner Hut, you now have the option to climb the Schwarzenstein, which was missed on the first opportunity. What choices indeed!

If you climbed the Schwarzenstein on the first opportunity, my recommendation would be to descend to the Greizer Hut via the Floitenkees glacier. This is now quite a difficult journey, but it is a very good exercise in glacier travel, route finding and general mountain skills.

For those who missed out on climbing the Schwarzenstein, the recommendation is that you follow the route description from the Schwarzenstein Hut across the Schwarzenstein Sattel (3143m) to the Berliner Hut, with the option to climb the Schwarzenstein (3369m).

The commentary and cautionary notes for each of the above routes are as described for Stage 4 of the ZRR.

On the Schwarzenstein (3369m)

For route description from the Schwarzenstein Hut to the Berliner Hut or Greizer Hut, see ZRR Stage 4.

Schwarzenstein Hut to the Greizer Hut alternative route

See ZRR Stage 4A. Reverse the route description across the Trippachsattel (3028m) and descend across the complex Floitenkees glacier generally as follows.

Tackle up on leaving the hut and head back to the left edge of the Trippachsattel with its large metal border marker post. Here, looking down the glacier and across the void in the general direction towards the Grosser Loeffler, you will be able to see the foot of the Westliche Floitenspitze ridge. Head for this, proceeding down the crevassed slope of the Floitenkees glacier. Round the foot of the buttress, but do not linger here and move at pace as the area is prone to stonefalls. Thereafter, once clear of the buttress, pick your way through the crevasses down

On the Schwarzenstein (3369m) looking towards the peaks: Olperer (left) Gefrorene-Wand-Spitzen (centre), Hoher Riffler (right)

Negotiating old moraines by ladder at the foot of the Schwarzensteinkees glacier

the glaciated slope, heading for the rocks immediately ahead. Be careful here as there is a lot of glacial rubble until you reach easier ground and the marked path to the Greizer Hut. Allow around 5hr and avoid the route in less than good weather.

Bad weather option

Should you be unfortunate to have poor weather at the Schwarzenstein Hut, which would make any of the above glacier crossings dangerous, your only safe option is to descend into the Ahrntal valley to Luttach. Get the local bus service to Brunneck, then the regional train service to Brixen, Sterzing and the Brenner pass and continue across the Austrian-Italian border to Innsbruck, a rather tedious but safe journey that will take the whole day.

HUT DIRECTORY

At Furtschaglhaus, with the Grosser Moeseler in the distance

Hut descriptions and locations

The hut descriptions are derived from the Alpenverein Hut Directory Volume 1 Ostalpen (previously known as the 'Green Book'), as published by Rother of Munich, together with information available from various tourist offices and that published by the OeAV, DAV, AVS and the huts themselves.

Other comments and observations are entirely those of the author.

More and more of the Zillertal huts are developing internet websites and email addresses, which means readers can now make reservations online and check for up-to-date information on the huts by visiting the following sites:

www.alpenverein.at/britannia
www.alpenverein.at/huetten
www.alpsonline.org/guest/login
www.bergsteigen.com
www.Alpenverein.de
www.mayrhofen.at/en/stories/peter-habeler-route

Abbreviations		
B	Beds	As in bedrooms
M	*Matratzenlager*	As in dormitory-style accommodation
N	*Notlager*	As in the winter room or other available space but more commonly known as 'sleeping with the furniture'

Day walks from Mayrhofen

All the huts mentioned, apart from those in the South Tirol of Italy, connect with the main Zillertal valley and the resort town of Mayrhofen. This means that all the huts are accessible as day walks, starting and finishing at the railway-cum-bus station in Mayrhofen, for visitors based in Mayrhofen wanting a mountain experience. See individual hut descriptions for details.

Berliner Hut (2042m)

Location	Located at the head of the Zemmgrund valley
Transport	From Mayrhofen, Postbus 4102 to Breitlahner: 09:05/09:35/10:05/10:35
Connections	Greizer Hut 6–8hr, Furtschaglhaus 6–7hr; Schwarzenstein Hut 7–8hr; Breitlahner 3hr
Owner	DAV Sektion Berlin
Open	Early June to early October
Facilities	75B/102M/20N Excellent restaurant and toilet facilities complete with showers and hot water. Everything you would expect from the biggest hut in the Zillertal
Excursions	Berliner Spitze (3254m) 4–5hr, Schwarzenstein (3369m) 6hr, Schwarzsee (2472m) 1½hr
Address	Berliner Hut, Maike Koeck and Florian Illmer, Zemmgrund 282, A-6295 Mayrhofen, Zillertal, Austria
Tel	Hut (0043) 5286 20062; mobile (0043) 664 88 78 70 25
Email	info@berlinerhuette.at

On 28 July 1879 the Berliner Hut had the distinction of being the first hut to open in the Zillertal; thereafter, the hut was subsequently enlarged in 1885. By 1890 the hut was proving to be much too small, thanks to its ever-increasing popularity, and an entirely new hut was built in 1892, which in turn was also extended in 1911 to its present status.

The Berliner Hut is a magnificent five-storey build-ing of medieval proportions and more akin to a moun-tain lodge fit for royalty than a hut for would-be alpinists. The hut reflects the great wealth and pride of the German Alpine Club at the turn of the twentieth century.

Over the years, the hut has remained virtually unchanged, except for the addition of modern plumbing and electricity, and is protected by the European Union as a building of historical significance. The reception hall has a very grand timber staircase complete with a decora-tive timber chandelier, which would have been adorned with oil lamps in the days before electricity. Adjacent walls are graced with important dignitaries: with long-deceased *Huettenwirts* and DAV Presidents.

The hut's lofty corridors of creaking timbers are individually styled, indicating various different ranks and social status. The timber panelling reflects an era long past when the hut was used by the Austrian Royal family, the military and the political elite as a hunting lodge as well as a base for alpine excursions.

The centre piece of the hut remains the substantial dining room, which in years gone by would have doubled as a ballroom and boomed to the sounds of Strauss

*Berliner Hut
dining room*

and brass bands amid much beer drinking and revelry. Naturally, the exhausted ladies would have then retired to the sanctuary of the adjacent and very private ladies' room. Can't blame them. Who would have wanted to stay in a room full of cigar- and pipe-smoking fellas?

More recently, the hut was used as a base to train the elite forces of the German Army during World War 2. A small memorial below the hut commemorates the members of the DAV Sektion Berlin, civilian and military, who perished during the conflict of both wars.

It is a fabulous, very grand and memorable place and worthy of a visit by all.

Berliner Hut DAV Sektion Berlin War Memorial

Day walk from Mayrhofen

From Mayrhofen railway station, by Postbus 4102 to and from Breitlahner. Outward: 07:35/08:35/09:05/09:35. Return: 13:55/14:55 then every half hour up to 18:25

This is a super day out in the mountains but best to be on your way early to get the most from the day and to enjoy the magnificence and grandeur of the Berliner Hut.

The walk can be split into three sections, namely forest, meadow and alpine, each with their own distinct type of scenery.

From the Breitlahner Bergbauernhof hotel, the sign-post declares the Berliner Hut is 3hr distant following directions for Route 523. The route follows a graded single-track service-road-cum-track that leads initially through the Zemmgrund valley to the colourful farm at Klausenalm (refreshments available). From here on, the track levels out to provide very pleasant easy alpine walking that embraces chocolate-box scenery of forest and high pasture until it cranks up, ending at the Grawandalm (refreshments available). **2hr** The route now steepens significantly, climbing through a series of zigzags for about 1km before gradually levelling out. From here on, the route continues on a section of concreted road to a bend in the road with a waterfall. Pause a while here – just above the road, out of reach of people and animals are many Edelweiss flowers – before continuing to the colourful Alpenrose Gasthof (refreshments and overnight accommodation available). There is excellent pastoral scenery hereabouts, but it is still a little too low to see the surrounding peaks. **Approx. 3hr**

The graded track ends here and continues as a mountain trail. From here on, the path steepens and climbs through diminishing woodland, zigzagging here and there on an uneven, rocky trail. About 10min below the magnificent Berliner Hut, the route passes the memorial to DAV Sektion Berlin members who perished during World War 1 and 2. **½hr to the hut**

Allow 2½–3hr for the return journey to Breitlahner.

Dominikus Hut Alpengasthof (1805m)

Location	Situated just above the bus terminus at the Schlegeisspeicher reservoir
Transport	Postbus 4102 to Mayrhofen 08:40/09:40/10:10/10:40/11:10/11:40
Connections	Pfitscherjochhaus 3hr; Olperer Hut 2–3hr; Friesenberghaus 3hr
Owner	Private
Open	Late May to early October
Facilities	50B/40M Good restaurant and toilet facilities, which can be expected from a hut that is more of a hotel than a hut
Address	Family Lapp, Dominikus Hut, Dornauberg 104, A 6292 Finkenberg, Austria
Tel	Hut (0043) 664 732 96 939
Email	info@dominikushuette.at

The original Dominikus Hut was built in 1883 by the D und OeAV, funded by Hermann Dominikus of Sektion Prague, hence the hut's name. When Herr Dominikus passed away, the hut was sold to the Eder family from Breitlahner; they in turn sold the hut to mountain guide

Dominikus Hut

Hans Hoerhager, who ran the hut from 1890 until the end of World War 1 when, for unexplained reasons, the hut burnt down. Hoerhager rebuilt the hut and handed its management to his daughter Lisl. Following the Treaty of St-Germain, the Dominikus Hut became part of Italian territory, with its owners requiring a passport to get to their own property. Common sense prevailed when the border was relocated to the Pfitscherjoch.

The original Dominikus Hut was lost during the construction of the Schlegeis reservoir when the valley was flooded in July 1973. The new larger Dominikus Hut you see today was built to replace the old hut.

While the Dominikus Hut does not feature on any of the tours in this guide, it is worth knowing about when things don't go exactly to plan, more so when the weather dictates events and participants need somewhere to stay.

The Dominikus Hut is easy to get to, is very comfortable and provides sanctuary when things get tough.

Edelraut Hut (2545m)

Location	Situated on the broad saddle of Eisbruggjoch
Transport	Postbus to/from Lappach and Neveser Stausee reservoir 3hr
Connections	Hochfeiler Hut 6hr, Nevesjoch Hut 4–5hr
Owner	CAI Sektion Brixen
Other names	Rifugio Passo Ponte di Ghiaccio, Eisbruggjoch Hut
Open	Mid June to late October
Facilities	18B/32M/8N Good restaurant facilities with modern toilet facilities that can feel a bit cramped when the hut is full
Excursions	Hochfeiler (3510m) 6hr, Hoher Weisszint (3371m) 6hr
Address	Herr Michael and Anton Weissteiner, Edelraut Hut, Ortnerweg 2 via Ortner, I-39030 Lappach, Autonome Provinz Bozen, Suedtirol, Italy
Tel	Hut (0039) 0474 653 230; WhatsApp Phone (0039) 340 660 4738
Email	info@edelrauthuette.it

This splendid hut was built in 2016 to replace the old hut but it continues to reflect everything that one could wish for when staying at a mountain hut: it is warm, friendly and welcoming for all the right reasons in the *Gemutlichkeit* tradition.

The new hut reflects a long history of over 100 years of the Edelraut Hut. The original hut was built in 1908 by the Vienna Mountaineering Club, who named the hut after a flower and a district of Vienna. Ownership of the hut passed to the DAV on amalgamation with the OeAV in 1873. In 1914 the hut was then renamed the Eisbruggjoch – despite there being not the slightest amount of ice anywhere near the hut. During World War 1 the hut was closed before being forfeited to Italy in 1919. After being transferred to the CAI, the hut reopened in 1925 as the Rifugio Passo Ponte di Ghiaccio.

During the 1920s smuggling was rife and it became so severe that the Italian authorities issued a warning in 1927: of 20–30 years in jail for those caught trafficking wine, schnapps, cigarettes, gold and money.

It is important to remember that Austria at that time was in financial ruin, having lost two-thirds of its land mass, including all of the South Tirol and 72 D&OAV huts. It was at this time that the Italian military started occupying all the huts along the South Tirol border.

A period of peace and quiet followed until 1939 when the Italian dictator Mussolini declared that all German-speaking Sudtirolese should leave Italy for good unless they embraced the Italian language and way of life. As a result, many Sudtirolese folk were forcibly evicted from their homes, including the then *Huettenwirtin*, Magdelena, with her daughter, Paula, and son, Sepp. The photograph in the dining room shows the family at Brixen railway station leaving for Germany and heading to an unknown fate and the eventual World War 2.

Situated on the broad saddle of Eisbruggjoch, the hut occupies a wonderful position with excellent view overlooking the Eisbrugg See alpine tarn to the south-west and the peaks of the Hoher Weisszint to the north. The Neveserjoch Hut, better known as the Alte Chemnitzer Hut, can clearly be seen across the valley to the east, perched on a similar broad saddle of the Nevesjoch, from where the hut gets its name, some 3–5hr distant.

During World War 2, the hut was closed and occupied by the Italian military, who plundered the hut and caused needless damage. Towards the end of the war the hut was strafed several times by the advancing American Air Force, which left what remained of the hut in ruins. Re-construction of the hut took place during 1949–51, mostly by the Italian military as recompense for the damage they had caused.

All was fine up to 1964 when the South Tirol question was again on the political agenda, which resulted in the Italian military occupying all the huts on the Sudtirol border. The army eventually vacated in 1972 and the hut reopened in 1976. The winter room and external *Matratzenlager* (mixed dormitory) was rebuilt and opened in 1980; however, the hut was forced to close in 1985 after losing most of its roof during a storm. Sadly, nothing lasts forever, and the old hut with its creaking timbers was demolished in 2015, giving way to a new hut and adding another chapter to the history of the Edelraut Hut. Like its predecessor, this is a splendid hut for all the right reasons in every sense of the *Gemuetlichkeit* (homely) tradition.

Friesenberghaus (2498m)

Location	Located on the southern flank of the Hoher Riffler (3168m)
Transport	Mayrhofen via Breitlahner and Ginzling. Postbus 4102 times from Mayrhofen: 08:35/09:05/09:35/10:05/10:35/11:35; from Schlegeis: 10:10/10:40/11:10/11:40/12:40/13:40/14:40 then every half hour up to 18:10
Connections	Olperer Hut 3hr, Gams Hut 10–12 hr, Schlegeis 2hr
Owner	DAV Sektion Berlin
Open	Mid June to end of September
Facilities	13B/33M Good restaurant and toilet facilities. Rooms are very tasteful and furnished in the rustic style of old Austria. Debit card payment facility
Address	Susanne Albertini and Florian Schranz, Friesenberghaus, Dornauberg 101, A-6295 Ginzling, Austria
Tel	Hut (0043) 0676 749 7550
Email	friesenberghaus@gmx.at

Named after the historic German town of Friesenberg, Friesenberghaus is a very pleasant, traditional three-storey stone-built hut that has the honour of being the highest hut in the Austrian Zillertal at just a tad short of 2500m. Not surprisingly, the hut has a commanding view over the main peaks of the Zillertal and Zamsergrund valley.

The hut has a very interesting if somewhat tragic history. Built in 1921 as a private enterprise by the Jewish community, the hut was then subsequently enlarged between 1928 and 1930. Then in 1938, as dark clouds

Friesenberghaus

passed over Europe, the then Jewish *Huettenwirt* had the unenviable position of wardening the hut at a time when the hut and its environs were being used to train the very best of the German Army's elite mountain troops.

A plaque in the hallway commemorates the assistance of Jewish climbers during this period:

'In the memory of the Jewish climbers and their friends who between 1923 and 1930 built the Friesenberghaus. In 1968 it was handed over by the survivors to the Berlin Sektion of the DAV as thanks for their resistance against the expulsion of Jewish climbers in 1933 from the DAV and OeAV.'

In 1980 Sektion Berlin presented the plaque to the surviving 150 members of the Donau Mountaineering Club on the 50th-year celebrations of the Friesenberghaus.

Unfortunately, after World War 2, attempts to warden the hut proved too difficult, and the hut was abandoned and plunged into a state of dereliction.

Around 1964 the Schmitt family from Heidelberg took possession of the hut and gradually restored it to its present *Gemuetlichkeit* (homely) condition. They are owed our unconditional thanks for having been such fine custodians of this splendid place.

Just outside the hut a bronze memorial plaque is mounted on a natural stone column. Presented by the DAV in 2001 to celebrate 80 years of the Friesenberghaus, the plaque proclaims against intolerance and hate.

Day walk from Mayrhofen

Bus 4102 service from Mayrhofen 08:35/09:05/09:35 to the terminus at Schlegeisspeicher. Return service: 16:10/16:40/17:40/18:10.

From the restaurant, walk down the road in the direction of Mayrhofen for a short distance to a signpost indicating the way to the Dominikus Hut and Friesenberghaus. Pick up the trail and follow Route 532 generally in a N direction first through the forest and scrub vegetation. After about 1hr you will reach the farm building used for storing hay at Friesenbergalm; this is a pleasant place for a short break. **1hr** The route now cranks up a few degrees and follows a good but rocky path through the hanging valley below the steep, rocky slopes of Gamsleiten. Midway you will cross the Lapenkarbach stream, and thereafter the route continues along a gradually steepening series of zigzags that traverses the slopes under the Friesenberghaus on the 2300m contour. After a further short distance, round a corner and the Friesenberghaus reveals itself. **3hr**

Furtschaglhaus (2295m)

Location	Located on the south-west flank of the Grosser Moeseler with wall-to-wall mountain scenery and a stunning view of the Hochfeiler
Transport	Mayrhofen via Schlegeis, Breitlahner, Ginzling Postbus 4102 times from Mayrhofen: 08:35 / 09:05 / 09:35 / 10:05 / 10:35 / 11:35 / 12:35; from Schlegeis: 10:10 / 10:40 / 11:10 / 11:40 / 12:40 / 13:40 then every half hour to 18:10
Connections	Olperer Hut 5–6hr, Berliner Hut 6hr, Pfitscherjochhaus 4–5hr
Owner	DAV Sektion Berlin
Open	Mid June to end of September
Facilities	56B/64M/12N Good restaurant and toilet facilities. Token-operated showers
Address	Katja lucas and Gunner Wehhahn, Dornauberg Nr 123, A-6295 Ginzling, Austria
Tel	Hut (0043) 6818 4218751
Email	info@furtschaglhaus.at

The hut occupies a commanding setting with wall-to-wall mountain scenery among some of the Zillertal's finest mountains, particularly the Zillertal's first and second highest peaks, the Hochfeiler (3510m) and Grosser Moeseler (3480m).

It goes without saying that there are no easy routes on these mountains. From the hut's terrace, aspiring alpinists may ponder an ascent of the Hochfeiler's classical 500m-high *Norwand* (north face), first climbed over three days in 1887, now rarely climbed except in winter.

The hut was constructed in 1889 and opened with just 20 beds and a small room for ladies. Extended in 1893 and 1912, the hut then remained virtually unchanged for almost 50 years except for the addition of electricity and modern plumbing. The hut was enlarged in 1968 and again in 1990 to its present size and for the

2000 millennium celebrations it had a cosmetic makeo-
ver, including a refurbished dormitory, *Gastestube* (dining room), kitchen and washrooms.

Furtschaglhaus

Day walk from Mayrhofen

Bus 4102 to and from Schlegeis reservoir bus terminus. From Mayrhofen
railway station: 08:35/09:05/09:35/10:05. Return service: 15:40 then every
half hour to 18:10

From the restaurant adjacent to the reservoir, with your
back to Mayrhofen, walk along the road for 200 metres
to the large car parking area where the road ends (signpost for Furtschaglhaus, Olperer Hut, Pfitscherjochhaus).

Follow Route 502, better known as the Central
Alpine Way, SE along the shoreline of the man-made lake
until it comes to a natural end. **1½hr**

Here there are excellent retrospective views across the reservoir towards the Olperer and Hoher Riffler, where sharp eyes will be able of pick out both the Olperer Hut and Friesenberghaus.

Continue to follow the service track, where after a short distance a signpost indicates the way uphill to Furtschaglhaus. Turn NE and follow the zigzagging trail, first through scrub vegetation then along a rocky path, to Furtschaglhaus. **1½hr** There are excellent views of the Hochfeiler.

Gams Hut (1916m)

Location	Located at the foot of the Grinbergspitze east ridge with a commanding view over Mayrhofen and the Zillertal valley
Transport	To Mayrhofen via Finkenberg or Ginzling. From Finkenberg Postbus 4104 service: 09:16/09:51/10:51/11:51; from Ginzling Postbus 4102 service: 10:29/10:59/11:29/12:59
Connections	Friesenberghaus 8–10hr
Owner	DAV Sektion Otterfing
Open	Mid June to end of September
Facilities	40M/10N Excellent restaurant and toilet facilities
Address	Gamshuette, Corina Epp, Brunnhaus 417, A-6292 Finkenberg im Zillertal, Austria
Tel	Hut (0043) 664 428 2969
Email	info@gamshuette.at

This hut has the distinction of being the lowest hut on the Zillertal Rucksack Route. Despite its lowly stature, the hut enjoys a commanding view across the Zemmgrund valley towards the peak of the Dristner, where my close friend Helmut Meier died in a fateful fall.

Those with sharp eyes will be able to locate the hut from Mayrhofen; its gleaming roof makes it clearly visible on the east ridge of the Grinbergspitze, which dominates the Zillertal valley.

The Gams Hut is a pleasant two-storey building with a splendid copper roof that projects a golden glow when the sun hits it from the right direction. The hut is easily accessible from Finkenberg and Ginzling, making it a popular day excursion for valley walkers, who pack the hut's terrace during the day. However, once the sun has gone down, it's not unusual to have the run of the place, as the only residents will be those starting or finishing the ZRR.

The hut, known then as the Grunerberg Hut, was built in 1927 as a private enterprise. It was purchased by the DAV Sektion Kurmack from the northern German province of Prussia before being transferred after World War 2 to DAV Sektion Berlin in 1956, who in turn passed the hut to DAV Sektion Otterfing, the present owners.

Modernised and extended in 1988, the hut has two dining rooms whose walls are liberally decorated with the horns of the goat-sized chamois mountain antelope, trophies from various hunting trips, hence the hut's name. The original dining room also has a bar, which will be a welcome sight for many beer drinkers who prefer to stand rather than sit, particularly those celebrating the completion of the ZRR.

Day walk from Mayrhofen

You have a choice of routes: by way of Finkenberg or Ginzling.

For **Finkenberg**, start from Mayrhofen railway station by picking up the trail of footpath #12, heading N, passing Gasthof Clara then turning left (W) to cross the Ziller river. Once across the river turn left, heading SW upstream on Route #12 across various pasture and pleasant alpine-type meadows into the charming little village of Finkenberg. Now head more S across the picturesque, gravity-defying Teufelsbruecke (Devil's Bridge) over the Tuxbach river and gorge. Thereafter, follow the steep, zigzagging trail on Route 533 through the Brunnhauswald forest to the Gams Hut. **4hr** Return by the same route or alternatively descend to the village of Ginzling.

Alternatively, by 4104 bus from Mayrhofen to Finkenberg (Innerberg-Persal) 08:45/09:40/10:40

From the bus stop, follow the main road for around 300 metres towards Krapfen, then turn left onto the forest access road. Two signposts point towards the Gams Hut: one says 2½hr and the other says 3hr. Continue following the long zigzags until you reach a sign for the Gams Hut pointing to a vague track going off to the left. Ignore this, as the track is very wet, and continue along the forest trail. Negotiate a stream then at the signpost turn right, heading uphill. Continue along the bridleway-type track until you reach Grindbergalm farm; here the route goes left or right. Continue right along the bridleway, cross a number of streams, then at around the 1700m contour a signpost points right. Follow this vague, wet and overgrown path until it emerges on a little col and at signpost indicating that the hut is a further 5min away.

In descent, follow the Hermann Hecht Weg on Route 533, pleasant walking through the Gamsberg forest, until it reaches the forest service road. The route then crosses a number of zigzags until reaching the 1100m contour and the main road at Dornau. Follow this to Finkenberg and the bus stop at Persal for the bus back to Mayrhofen; alternatively, you can walk back.

While the ascent is given as 2½hr, 3hr is more realistic. Allow 2½hr for the descent.

For **Ginzling**, start from Mayrhofen railway station and take Postbus 4102 to Ginzling (bus times: 09:05/09:35/10:05). Get off the bus at Schrambach, then once across the Zemmbach river, head N for about 1km (signpost). Thereafter, head NW, following the steep, zigzagging forest trail that climbs a long way, almost 1000m, through woodland to the hut. **3hr**

Note that while you are in Ginzling, the Alte Ginzling Hotel has the best *Gebirgesforelle* (grilled or poached trout) in the entire Zillertal. Enjoy!

Postbus 4102 Ginzling to Mayrhofen: 16:25/16:55/17:55/18:25

Gasthof Stein (1555m)

Location	Midway between Pfitch and Pfitscherjoch
Connections	Pfitscherjochhaus 20min by taxi or 1hr on foot
Owner	Private
Address	Family Kasslatter, I-39049 Pfitsch Val di Vizze, Stein-Sasso nr 95, Sud Tirol-Alto Adige, Italy
Tel	(0039) 472 630 130

Gasthof Stein is not so much a hut but rather a collection of farm buildings with the main house doubling as a *Gasthof* (guest house). It is a typical large chalet-type building that has seen so little change over many years that it is almost a museum, reflecting the bygone era of the old Sud Tirol. The reason for its inclusion is that it is quite close to the Pfitscherjoch and is a viable alternative to staying at the large, impersonal Pfitscherjochhaus, being just a 20min taxi ride away by Mietwagen Steinert tel 0039 472 630 121 or mobile 340 145 6313.

However, making a reservation can be problematic as the owners do not speak any English and their German is very much of a strong Sud Tirol dialect. Fortunately, the family usually employ an English-Italian-German-speaking intern during the summer to help out since the Gasthof is located on the Meran–Munich long-distance trail. This is a memorable place to stay and is highly recommended, if you don't mind going out of your way.

Geraer Hut (2326m)

Location	Situated on a level platform at the upper edge of alpine meadows overlooking the Stubai Alps; hemmed in at the rear by the sheer rock walls of the Schrammacher and Fussstein
Transport	From Innsbruck by regional train service to Steinach am Brenner at 09:22/10:22/11:22, then by Postbus to Touristenrast guest house in the Valsertal valley at 11:45/13:35, a journey time of around 1hr. Note that there is no bus service on Sundays. Taxi service available from Steinach railway station: 20min ride by taxi. Tel Wipptal Taxi 0043 664 1223055. See below for directions from Touristenrast
Connections	Olperer Hut 6–7hr, Pfitscherjochhaus 6–7hr, Landshuter 6hr Note that the path to the Pfitscherjochhaus has collapsed approximately halfway to the hut. The

	subsequent diversion adds almost 2hr to the journey. See notes for the Zillertal South Tirol Tour
Owner	DAV Sektion Landshut
Open	Mid June to end of September, depending on the weather
Facilities	80B/100M/12N Good restaurant and toilet facilities with hot water and showers. Drying room, internet facility. *Seilbahn* (goods hoist) rucksack delivery service
Address	Geraer Hut, Herr Arthur Lanthaler, Vals 24b/1, A-6154 Vals-Tirol, Austria
Tel	Hut (0043) 0676 9610 303; Mobile (0043) 0664 5106 830
Email	info@geraerhuette.at

From the Touristenrast Gasthof (no overnight accommodation), continue up the Valsertal valley to the end of the service track road to the *Seilbahn* (goods hoist) (signpost). **¾hr** From here on, follow the well-marked path through the forest for a about 2hr to farm buildings and an alm. Once in open landscape, the trail crosses two footbridges and a small gorge with a river not too distant from the hut.

Good path all the way on long, looping zigzags. **3–4hr**

The hut is managed by the husband-and-wife team of Arthur and Katharina Lanthaler. Arthur is by profession a *Bergfuehrer* (mountain guide), which is very helpful should you need advice about the mountains and the area in general. The hut is named after the north-east German town of Gera and occupies a commanding position high above the Valsertal valley with good views over the Valsertal and Wipptal valleys towards the Stubai Alps. To the rear the hut is greatly hemmed in by the dominating peaks of the Schrammacher (3410m) and the Fusstein (3380m).

During World War 2 the hut was occupied by German military engineers as the area above the hut was mined for chrome molybdenum, an important mineral in the production of chromoly steel, used to build battle tanks. Safe in the Valsertal valley, protected by the

Geraer Hut

mountains, the mine was worked by a workforce of 143, which comprised 34 Germans, 9 French, 27 Italians and 75 *Ostarbeiters*, namely slave workers from German-occupied Ukraine and Poland.

As the Allies and the American Airforce advanced in 1944 across the Brenner pass into Austria, several attempts were made to bomb the difficult-to-get-to mine but with little success. The mountain, however, had other ideas and on 11 November 1944, a huge avalanche swept the barracks and all the staging off the mountain, killing 17 *Ostarbeiters* and seriously injuring 23 others. A second avalanche thundered down off the Schrammacher two days later, completing the mine's destruction, this time without loss of life.

Today all that remains of these sad times are a number of steel pylons, general relics of the barracks scattered about and a padlocked gate to the mine entrance.

After the war, Gera became part of the DDR of East Germany, and Sektion Gera lost ownership of the hut. Lying abandoned until 1956, the hut passed into the ownership of the Bavarian DAV Sektion Landshut. who have been fine custodians of the hut ever since.

Built in 1895, architecturally this is a charming, traditional two-storey hut with walls clad with larch shingles topped off with a bright copper roof. Internally, everything is made of wood: timber-panelled walls, boarded floors, a decorative ceiling, tables, chairs – even the water stand is made of wood. The creaking timbers and gentle soft furnishings all add to a very charming, cosy atmosphere, making this a brilliant hut for all the right reasons.

Greizer Hut (2226m)

Location	Located on the western flank of the Griesfeld, with a commanding view of the Floitenkees glacier and peaks of the Schwarzenstein, this one of the best situated huts in the Zillertal
Transport	To Ginzling then Postbus to Mayrhofen. Shuttle minibus taxi service available to/from the hut's *Seilbahn* (goods hoist). Tel Floitental Huetten Taxi 0664 1029354
Connections	Kasseler Hut 6hr; Gruene Wand Haus 6hr; Schwarzenstein Hut 5hr; Berliner Hut 6–8hr
Owner	DAV Sektion Greiz
Open	End of June to end of September
Facilities	24B/52M/14N Excellent restaurant and basic but adequate toilet facilities that can be a little cramped when the hut is full. Drying Room
Excursions	Grosser Loeffler 5–6hr; Schwarzenstein 6–7hr
Address	Herr Herbert and Irmi Schneeberger, Oberbichl 769, A-6184 Ramsau, Zillertal, Austria
Tel	(0043) 5282 3211; Mobile (0043) 664 1405003
Email	greizerhuette@aon.at
Website	www.greizerhuette.at, www.alpenverein-greiz.de

Constructed in 1897, and subsequently enlarged in 1905, 1927 and then again in 1972 and 1974, the hut belongs to Sektion Griez, a former Sektion of the East German DAV.

Greizer Hut

This is quite an old but superb little hut which has an ambience of *Gemuetlichkeit* (homeliness) as soon as you pass through its front door. The *Alte Gastestube* (old dining room) is adorned with the Greiz coat of arms and portraits of *Huettenwirts* throughout the hut's golden age. And the views from the hut's terrace and dining room towards the Floitenkees glacier are exceptional, with wall-to-wall mountain scenery providing a suitable backdrop for rest and relaxation.

The hut was originally built to provide easy access to the Floitenkees glacier and the routes across the Schwarzenstein into the then South Tirol. With the retreat of the glacier over the years, individuals may well wonder why the hut was not built higher up. It is worth remembering that in 1900 the Floitenkees glacier was just 100 metres from the hut's front door.

This is also one of the few remaining huts that partly relies on both a *Seilbahn* (goods hoist) and a *Haflinger* horse for hauling its supplies and provisions up from

Ginzling. These fine beasts of burden are renowned for their size and strength, having been bred over the centuries to cope with steep alpine terrain.

The winter room was added in 1926 and, if you are lucky enough to get billeted in this annexe, these wonderful Haflinger horses will keep you company, along with the winter room's other smaller four-pawed creatures that will enjoy foraging through your rucksack and other belongings if you forget to store your gear off the floor.

Day walk from Mayrhofen

From Mayrhofen railway station, Postbus 4102 service to/from Ginzling: at 08:35/09:05/09:35/10:05.

From Ginzling take the Floitental shuttle taxi service (tel 0664 102 9354) to the *Seilbahn* at Ausserer Keesboden, an area much used for hunting the long-horned steinbok, better known as the ibex.

Thereafter, follow Route 521 along a rocky track that climbs initially quite gradually but then steepens considerably, following a rocky, zigzagging trail to the hut. **2hr**

Hochfeiler Hut (2710m)

Location	Situated on the southern flank of the Hochfeiler with a level platform hewn out of the rock overlooking the Gilder Ferner glacier
Transport	There are no easy valley connections to or from this hut
Connections	Pfitscherjochhaus 6hr, Edelraut Hut 3hr
Owner	AVS Sektion Sterzing
Other names	Rifugio Gran Pilastro
Open	Mid of June to mid September

Facilities	88M in rooms of different sizes. Good restaurant and toilet facilities; hot water and token-operated showers; drying room This is a very busy hut due to its proximity to the Hochfeiler; you are strongly advised to reserve beds even if travelling on your own
Excursions	Hochfeiler 3hr, Hochferner Spitze 6hr
Address	Herr Andreas Hernegger, Hochfeiler Hut, I-39040 Pfitsch, Italy
Tel	Hut (0039) 5226 2218 or 0472 646071; WhatsApp phone (0039) 340 793 1869
Email	info@hochfeilerhuette.it

Hochfeiler Hut

Situated at just over 2700m, this unsurprisingly very robust, three-storey stone hut is built to withstand the elements. Indeed, when the hut first opened, the then Gilder Ferner glacier passed within 100 metres of the hut's front door.

The original hut, which opened in August 1881, was known as the Wiener Hut, named after OeAV Sektion Vienna. During this period, in 1894, Sir Martin Conway passed through on his Grand Traverse of the Alps. After

World War 1 the hut passed into Italian hands, with its ownership being handed to the CAI Section Monza in 1922. The passing years witnessed a lean time, as most of the hut's occupancy was taken up by the Italian military. During World War 2 the hut was badly damaged by the American Air Force and suffered from general neglect and the ravages of the weather. With wartime damage repaired, the hut reopened in 1950, with further repairs taking place throughout the following decade. Similar to the other huts in the South Tirol, the Hochfeiler Hut witnessed smuggling and insurgency activity across the border with Austria, which led the Italian elite troops of the Alpini to blow up the hut in 1962, forcing it to close for the next 20 years.

The new hut, built much higher up the mountain, is relatively new and opened in 1986. For those with an interest in such things, the old foundations are still visible below the present hut, at the start of the zigzag path.

The dining room is very pleasant and has a commanding view down the Pfitschertal valley and a terrific view across the great void to the Austrian Stubai Alps. Those of you with binoculars should be able to locate the Becher Haus sitting on its rocky knoll. In the dining room hangs a photographic print of a painting of the then Wiener Hut in 1900 by the Victorian artist ET Compton. The painting was presented to the OeAV in 1966 and is displayed in the Alpine Museum in Innsbruck.

This is a very busy hut with most residents wanting to climb the highest peak in the Zillertal, the Hochfeiler (3510m), by the easiest of routes.

Kasseler Hut (2177m)

Location	Located at the foot of the Hintere Stangenspitze west ridge with a commanding view of the Grosser Loeffler
Transport	To/from Mayrhofen via the shuttle service from Europahaus/Gruene Wand Haus. Tel 0043 5285 63423 or mobile 0664 2006 596
Connections	Karl von Edel Hut 8–10hr, Greizer Hut 6hr
Owner	DAV Sektion Kassel
Open	Mid June to mid September
Facilities	22B/72M/10N Excellent restaurant and toilet facilities, including token-operated showers; *Seilbahn* (goods hoist) rucksack delivery service; drying room, internet facility; excellent daily weather forecast in English
Excursions	Wollbachspitze (3210m) 4hr, Gruene Wand Spitze (2946m) 3hr. Sektion Kassel has recently established a *Klettersteig* route just above the hut, on the Klettergarten to the Eurer Mandl. A more ambitious plan is for a *Klettersteig* route to be established on the Gruene Wand Spitze, which will be a great expedition once established.
Address	Anna and Lukas Decker, Kasseler Hut, Postfach 167, Stillupptal 970, A-6290 Mayrhofen, Austria
Tel	Hut (0043) 664 4016033
Email	kasseler-huette@alpenverein-kassel.de

This pleasant hut with its traditional timber-panelled interior was constructed in 1927 and subsequently enlarged in 1938, 1958 and 1982.

However, the hut's true heart lies elsewhere, as the original Kasseler Hut was built in 1877 in the Rieserferner Group of the South Tirol. The hut was then forfeited to Italy in 1919 after World War 1 as part of war reparations and is now known as the Rifugio Vedrette di Ries.

The Kasseler Hut is presently wardened by the husband-and-wife team of Anna and Lukas Decker, who are brilliant at making visitors welcome in the *Gemuetlichkeit* (homely) tradition, particularly with the all-important reading of the daily weather forecast.

Kasseler Hut

The hut is frequently used by various alpine schools and is often busy. Make enquiries with the hut or at the Europahaus tourist information centre in Mayrhofen to secure bed space.

Day walk from Mayrhofen and Stage 2 of Zillertal Rucksack Route

For those who wish to bypass the Edel Hut and the Stage 2 connection and go straight to the Kasseler Hut, the route description is as follows, similarly for those wanting to enjoy a day walk from Mayrhofen.

Make your way to to the Europahaus tourist information in the centre of Mayrhofen, a 5min walk from the railway station along Durster Strasse. A regular minibus service operates between here and the Gruene Wand Haus in the Stillupgrund valley.

From Gruene Wand Haus, follow signs and paths for the Kasseler Hut. **2hr** The first 1km of the trail is a continuation of the hut service road to the *Seilbahn* (material goods hoist). Here rucksacks can be placed on the *Seilbahn* for a modest fee (you will need to contact the hut using the field phone), allowing you a rucksack-free walk to the hut. From the *Seilbahn* the track heads through the Stapfenwald forest, following a zigzag trail overlooking the Sonntagskarbach river and gorge and eventually joining up with the route and path leading to the Edel Hut on the Seven Ridges trail, the Siebenschneidensteig (signpost). Thereafter, the route turns right and heads S over rocky, broken ground to the Kasseler Hut.

SHUTTLE MINIBUS SERVICE FROM MAYRHOFEN TO GRUENE WAND HAUS

The shuttle service to Gruene Wand Haus takes 40min to make the 16km journey and leaves the Europahaus tourist information centre in Mayrhofen at 08:00/08:30/10:00/11:00/15:00

Return service: 10:00/11:30/16:00

To reserve the shuttle service, tel 0043 5285 63423 or 0664 2006 596

Karl von Edel Hut (2238m)

Location	Located above Mayrhofen on the western slopes of the Ahornspitze
Transport	To Mayrhofen via the Ahornbahn cable car 1½hr, or Route 514 footpath and forest trail 3hr
Connections	Kasseler Hut 8–10hr
Owner	DAV Sektion Wuerzburg
Open	From mid June to end of September
Facilities	20B/60M/41N Excellent restaurant and toilet facilities, including showers. Internet facility. The hut is extremely busy during the day with day-trippers due to its close proximity to Mayrhofen via the Ahornbahn cable car
Excursions	Ahornspitze 2hr
Address	Siegfried and Gabi Schneeberger, Edel Hut, Ahorn Strasse 873e, A-6290 Mayrhofen, Tirol, Austria
Tel	(0043) 5285 62168; Mobile (0043) 664 915 4851
Email	info@apart-schneeberger.at
Website	www.dav-wuerzburg.de, www.edelhuette-dav.de

Named after the president of the German Alpine Club, the
Karl von Edel Hut was constructed in 1889 and remained
unchanged up to 1951 when it was totally destroyed following a devastating avalanche off the Ahornspitze, forcing it to close for the next six years. Once re-established,
the hut was enlarged in 1959, then refurbished in 1977
and again in 2001 to its present size.

Karl von Edel Hut

The hut, which is wardened by husband-and-wife
team Siegfried and Gabi Schneeberger, is a popular day
hut, being easily accessible from Mayrhofen. Many people make the short two-hour walk from the Ahornbahn
cable-car station, which boasts of being the largest cable-
car gondola in the Tirol, being akin to a double-decker
bus lying flat on its side. Once at the hut these visitors
will spend their time either sitting on the hut's terrace or
expending more energy by making the two-hour ascent
of the Ahornspitze (2973m).

However, once the sun dips below the horizon, it is
not unusual to have the run of the place, when you can

enjoy the hut's lofty position overlooking the bright lights of Mayrhofen and the Zillertal valley.

Day walk from Mayrhofen
See 'Stage 1 Mayrhofen to the Karl von Edel Hut'; allow 2hr from the cable-car station at Filzenalm, similarly for the return journey.

Landshuter Europa Hut (2693m)

Location	Located on a prominent part of the Tuxer Hauptkamm ridge, which marks the Austrian-Italian border with the Sud Tirol, with extensive views in all directions
Connections	From Brennersee on the Brenner pass 4hr; from Mayrhofen via Schlegeis 5hr; Pfitscherjoch 4hr, Geraer Hut 6–7hr, Olperer Hut 6–7hr
Owner	DAV Sektion Landshut and CAI Sektion Sterzing
Open	Early July to mid September
Facilities	28B/60M/10N Good restaurant and toilet facilities
Address	Familie Holzer, Landshuter Europa Hut, St Jakob 78, 39049 Pfitsch (Bz), Sudtirol, Italy
Tel	Hut Mobile (0039) 338 2124738, and (0039) 0472 630156
Email	info@europahuette.it; reservations via Florian Holzer on f.holzer@rolmail.net

Standing at the front door of one of the highest huts in the region, visitors are quickly reminded of how high the hut is and its strategic location with extensive views in all directions. To the north is the North Tirol and the peaks of the Inn valley, to the west are the mountains of the Stubai and Oetztal, to the east the Zillertal Alps, while to the south lie the lands of the Sud Tirol and Italian Alto Adige.

First established in 1889, the hut had limited success due to money problems. Ten years later, between 1889, 1902, and 1903, greatly aided by the opening of

*Landshuter Europa
Hut memorial plaque*

AN DEN DAV LANDSHUT
IN FREUNDSCHAFT – CON AMICIZIA

EUROPAHUTTE 11. 7. 1999
CAI ALTO ADIGE

the railway over the Brenner pass, the three-storey, buttressed stone building was built with quarters for personnel, a guest room and beds for 42 people.

The hut straddles the border with Italy. Some years ago, you knew that you were on the border because the window shutters on the Austrian side were painted red and white, while on the Italian side they were painted green and white. Sadly, this proud colour scheme has now gone, and today the border demarcation is noted in the entrance hallway by a large red sign that features a scary-looking eagle with the word Oesterreich in bold print. Outside on the Italian side you will find a simple white border post marker, which you could easily trip over.

After the annexation of the South Tirol in 1919 at the end of World War 1, the hut was occupied by the Italian military, evidence of which can be seen on the route to the Pfitscherjochhaus in the wide paved paths and buttressed walls built by the military engineers to ease the transportation of men and materials from the garrison at Pfitscherjoch to secure the Italian side of the border.

At the end of World War 2 the hut was abandoned and by the early 1950s it was semi-derelict. Some effort was put into cleaning up the hut, with modest renovations made around 1953; however, due to the difficult political situation of the era, with insurgency and smuggling, the hut was closed in 1966. Remember this was at a time when England was playing Germany in the World Cup.

Indeed, an attempt to blow up the hut in 1967 led to the Italian Army re-occupying it. Many more years of political wrangling over ownership and responsibility between Italy and Austria continued until a resolution of sorts was agreed and the hut finally reopened in 1972.

With the hut being located on the border, and with a history of two wars, ownership was always going to be contentious. A mountaineer's compromise was reached in 1989, stating the hut would be jointly owned by the Club Alpino Italiano Sektion Sterzing (Vipiteno) and the Deutscher Alpenverein Sektion Landshut, and the hut was renamed the Landshuter Europa Hut. A plaque in the hallway commemorates the event.

Presently, the hut is beginning to enjoy a bit of revival due to the establishment of the Tiroler Hoehenweg, the long-distance path from Merano to Mayrhofen, and the more recently established Peter Habeler Runde Tour, an extended version of the Olperer Runde Tour. Because of this and the general ease of access from Brenner or Schlegeis, the hut can be quite busy, particularly at weekends when it may be full.

The hut, as expected, is very well run and great effort is made in maintaining its historic tradition.

Nevesjoch Hut (2420m)

Location	Located in the broad saddle of the very prominent Nevesjoch
Connections	Neves-Stausee reservoir 5hr, Edelraut Hut 4–5hr, Schwarzenstein 8–9hr, Berliner Hut 8hr
Owner	CAI Sektion Bolzano (Bozen)
Other names	Rifugio Giovanni Porro, Alte Chemnitzer Hut
Open	Mid June to early October
Facilities	31B/30M/10N Good restaurant service but nominal toilet facilities that can feel cramped when the hut is full. However, the hut does have an excellent shower facility that would suit any hotel and is available for a modest fee
Excursions	Grosser Moeseler (3479m) 4hr
Address	Roland and Anna Gruber, Rifugio Giovanni Porro, Nevesjoch (Alte Chemnitzer) Hut, Frazione Lappago 1, I-39030 Lappago BZ, Italy
Tel	Hut (0039) 474 653 244, mobile (0039) 335 689 8111
Email	info@chemnitzerhuette.com

The original hut comprised a low wooden building of just two small rooms with a roof loft being built by the local OeAV Sektion Taufers during 1889–93; a modest extension was then added in 1895. Passing through in 1895 on his Grand Traverse of the Alps, Sir Martin Conway noted that they had to share the hut with a bunch of unfriendly local workmen, who were gruff and unsavoury characters, and lots of over-friendly mice.

Having no money, the local Sektion Taufers sought funds from the DAV Sektion Chemnitz who, unsurprisingly, when ownership was transferred to them, renamed the hut the Chemnitzer Hut, better known today as the Alte Chemnitzer Hut after the north German town of Chemnitz.

During World War 1 the hut was closed and occupied by the Austrian military. By 1916, due to the ravages

Nevesjoch Hut

of war, Sektion Chemnitz had been reduced to just 669 members. With the loss of the South Tirol, Sektion Chemnitz forfeited the hut, opting to build a new hut, the Neue Chemnitzer Hut, which opened in 1926 in the Piztal region of the Tirol.

Meanwhile, the Alte Chemnitzer-Nevesjoch Hut went through the same saga as all the other huts on the South Tirol border with Austria up to World War 2, which saw the hut being bombed and destroyed by the British and American air forces. By 1945 the hut was virtually in ruins.

A hut of sorts was built from the materials of the original hut and it managed to open in 1953. However, during the 1960s, smuggling was again rife across the South Tirol which saw the Italian military, the Alpini, taking up residence in the hut from 1962–1972. Left in a semi-derelict state once the army vacated, the hut managed to reopen in 1974.

Olperer Hut (2389m)

Location	Situated on the lower eastern slopes of the Olperer with a truly stunning view across the Schlegeis reservoir to the Hochfeiler and Grosser Moeseler
Transport	Valley connections to and from Mayrhofen via Schlegeis and Breitlahner. Postbus 4102 times from Mayrhofen: 09:05/09:35/10:05/10:35; from Schlegeis: 10:10/10:40/ 11:10/11:40/12:40/13:40/14:40 then every half hour to 18:10
Connections	Friesensenberg Haus 3hr, Furtschaglhaus 5hr, Geraer Hut 6hr, Pfitscherjochhaus 5hr
Owner	DAV Sektion Neumarkt
Open	From early June to early October
Facilities	60M in rooms 5x4,5x8/12N Good restaurant facilities and toilet facilities, token-operated showers, drying room.
Address	Katharina and Manuel Daum, Dornauberg 110, A-6295 Ginzling, Zillertal, Austria
Tel	(0043) 7203 46930; Mobile; (0043) 664 417 6566
Email	info@olpererhuette.de

This is a splendid hut with a commanding view over the Schlegeisspeicher reservoir towards the two highest peaks in the Zillertal range, the Hochfeiler (3510m) and the Grosser Moeseler (3480m).

The original hut, constructed in 1881 by Sektion Prague, was demolished by an avalanche and rebuilt in 1900 with donations from DAV Sektion Berlin, to whom its ownership was soon transferred. The hut was refurbished in 1931 and modestly extended in 1976, but it was badly damaged by a mud slide in 1998, forcing it to close for a season while the debris was removed and the hut was repaired.

Note, there is a current thinking that the relatively new suspension bridge near the hut was built as a simple tourist attraction; however, this is not the case. The bridge

Olperer Hut was built to span the chasm created by the rock and mud avalanche that almost destroyed the then hut.

Change came about when ownership of the hut was transferred from Sektion Berlin to the Bavarian Sektion Neumarkt in 2004. Full of vim and vigour, the new owners set about constructing the delightful Neumarkter Runde Panoramaweg in 2006. The new owners also quickly realised that the old hut was totally inadequate for the volume of traffic coming and going on the Zillertal Rucksack Route and the Peter Habeler and Olperer Runde Tours, plus the daily visitors from Mayrhofen. In 2006 the old hut, having served its purpose, was demolished and replaced by an entirely new hut, which opened in 2007 with an increased capacity for 60 people. The old winter room was similarly upgraded and refurbished to accommodate 12 people.

The new hut is a move away from traditional mountain hut design with its simple two-storey shoe-box-type structure and pitched roof. Internally, the hut is bright and clean and has an uncluttered ambience, the centrepiece being a full-width panoramic window overlooking the head of the Schlegeis reservoir and the fabulous peaks of the Hochfeiler and Grosser Moeseler.

With the advent of the road in the early 1970s, as a result of the Schlegeis hydroelectric project, the hut has become easily accessible from Mayrhofen, which means at weekends the hut is usually a very noisy full house. Participants are therefore advised to either avoid the weekends or to make a reservation, even if travelling alone.

The main excursion from the hut is the climb of the south-east ridge of the Olperer (3476m), the third-highest peak in the Zillertal. Thereafter, the hut occupies an important position on the Zillertal Rucksack Route and similarly for the Peter Habeler and Olperer Runde Tours.

Day walk from Mayrhofen

Bus from Mayrhofen to the bus terminus at Schlegeis reservoir and roadside restaurant

From Schlegeis reservoir follow the route as described for Stage 6 of the ZRR.

Alternatively, follow signs for the marginally longer but more scenically rewarding Neumarkter Runde Panoramaweg. **3hr**

From the restaurant, walk along the road for 200 metres to the large car parking area where the road ends (signpost for Furtschaglhaus, Pfitscherjochhaus and Panorama Hoehenweg). Pick up the track as directed, following Route 535, SW along a well-constructed path through the forest, with rhododendron and dwarf alpine pine bushes, for around 1hr to a footbridge across the Unterschrammachbach glacial river at 2127m. Cross the river and follow the track now more steeply NW into the large open combe and glacial basin of Hinterboden (signpost for Pfitscherjochhaus, Geraer Hut and Olperer Hut). **About 1½hr**

Bear right (N) on Route 502, better known as the Central Alpine Way, rounding the head of the combe to gain the rocky slopes of Schramerkopf. Follow the obvious rocky trail, traversing around the hillside below Schramerkopf on a path that has been painstakingly laid out, being part paved in places, until its natural conclusion at the Olperer Hut. **3hr**

There is excellent scenery throughout, particularly in the latter part of the walk, with fabulous views across the Schlegeis reservoir towards the Zillertal's high peaks.

Pfitscherjochhaus (2275m)

Location	Situated on the Italian south-west side of the Pfitscherjoch, about 500 metres from the Austrian border
Transport	To Schlegeis Stausee reservoir 2+hr then by Postbus 4102 to Mayrhofen: 10:10/10:40/11:10/11:40/12:40
Connections	Geraer Hut 6–7hr, Olperer Hut 6hr, Hochfeiler Hut 6–7hr
Owner	Private
Other names	Rifugio Passo di Vizze
Open	From late June to end of September
Facilities	30B/100M/12N Excellent restaurant and toilet facilities of a standard you would expect from a mountain hotel
Address	Josef Volgger, Pfitscherjochhaus, S.Jakob 103, I-39049 Pfitsch Val di Vizze BZ, Italy
Tel	Hut Mobile (0039) 333 8404587; Hut (0039) 0472 630119
Email	office@pfitscherjochhaus.com

This superbly sited hut was built in 1884 by Alois Rainer, a hotelier from St Jakob in Pfitsch. The hut was rebuilt in 1969 then extended in 1982 and modernised in 2000 and its excellent facilities are of a standard you would expect from a hotel.

During World War 1, the hut was garrisoned by the Austrian Army up until the armistice of 1918 when the whole of the South Tirol was forfeited to Italy. From

Pfitscherjochhaus

1919 the hut was garrisoned by the Alpine troops of the Italian Army, including the elite Alpini. Fearing an invasion by the Austrians trying to claim back the South Tirol, the Italians fortified the area; remnants of barrack buildings still exist just below the hut along with signs of the extensive trench systems. After the war, the military of both sides maintained an uneasy presence on the *Joch* (pass) to prevent counterinsurgency and the smuggling of goods, which was rife.

This situation continued until World War 2 when there was a friendly truce of sorts. However, after the war both sides resorted to their pre-1938 positions. This situation lasted for the next 20 years until 1966 when the Italian Army decided its only option was to blow up the hut. A further five years would pass before normal border crossing for the likes of you and me was allowed in 1971.

On the destruction of the hut and the departure of the military from Pfitscherjoch, the hut was eventually

given back to its rightful owners who then had the daunt-
ing task of suing for compensation. Many years would
again pass before the hut could be rebuilt, eventually
reopening in 1980.

Pfitscherjochhaus is a big hut that caters for all
mountain travellers, particularly trans-alp cyclists. The
main *Gastestube* (dining room) is self-service with all
sorts of meals on offer. The hut has *Matratzenlager* (dormitory) rooms but also proper bedrooms with en-suite
facilities. While this is a big hut, it is quite pleasant for the
short time you will be there.

Day walk from Mayrhofen

Bus from Mayrhofen to the bus terminus at Schlegeis reservoir and roadside
restaurant.
  Bus times from Mayrhofen: 09:05/09:35/10:50; from Schlegeis: 15:10
then every half hour until 18:10

From the restaurant adjacent to the reservoir, with your
back to Mayrhofen, walk along the road for 200 metres
to the large car park and rest area at Zammsgartterl-
Jausenstat where the road ends (signpost for
Furtschaglhaus, Olperer Hut, Pfitscherjochhaus).

Pick up the trail for this ancient trading route and
follow Route 524 along what was a paved, single-track
military road, heading SW along the right bank of the
Zamserbach river for 5km along the Via Alpina trail to
the charming Levitzalm farmstead (refreshments available). **2hr** Do not linger too long here, as there is still
some distance to go. Continuing as before, you can now
follow the service road or opt on and off, following various footpaths until you reach the Pftscherjoch with its
redundant police hut and nearby chapel, which sits on
the border with Italy. A large signpost welcomes you to
the Sud Tirol and the Alto Adige and eventually to the
Pfitscherjochhaus. **About ½–1hr**

Excellent views extend towards the Olperer and the Zamsergrund valley and Schlegeis and beyond to Mayrhofen.

Schwarzenstein Hut (3027m)

Location	Situated on a level rock promontory on the southern Italian side of the Trippachschneide ridge, it has the distinction of being the highest hut in the Zillertal
Transport Connections	There are no easy valley or hut connections from this hut To Luttach in the Rotbachtal valley 5hr, Nevesjoch-Chemnitzer Hut 8–10hr, Berliner Hut via Schwarzenstein 7–8hr, Greizer Hut via Floitenkees glacier 5hr
Owner	CAI Sektion Bruneck
Other names	Rifugio Vittorio Veneto al Sasso Nero
Open	From mid June to end of September. Of interest to ski tourers mid March to late April
Facilities	50M in rooms of 4, 6 and 10. Excellent restaurant and toilet facilities for the location and height
Excursions	Schwarzenstein 3hr, Floitenspitze 2hr, Grosser Loeffler 5–6hr, Grosser Moerchner 4–5hr
Address	Fr Margit Ainhauser, Gschleier 23, I-39010 Moelten, Sud Tirol, Italy
Tel	Hut (0039) 342 8038 586
Email	info@schwarzensteinhuette.com

This futuristic-looking, copper-clad angular building with its panoramic windows was built to replace the old hut which, despite having a European Union protection order, was demolished in 2016 after becoming unstable due to changes in the permafrost on which it sat. The new Schwarzenstein Hut, opened in July 2018, sits some 50m higher than the old hut, overlooking the Rieserferner mountains and the peaks of the Sexten Dolomites.

The new hut continues the long history of the original Schwarzenstein Hut, which was built in 1895 by the

Schwarzenstein Hut

D&OeAV Sektion Leipzig and opened with space for just 16 people. Thereafter, the hut was enlarged in 1896 and remained virtually unchanged, apart from the addition of modern plumbing and electricity.

As with the other huts along the South Tirol border, everything was fine up until the start of World War 1 when from 1914 to 1927 the hut was closed. After Austria's loss of the South Tirol at the Treaty of St-Germain in September 1919, the hut was taken over by the Italian military before being transferred to the Italian Alpine Club and Sektion Vittorio Veneto when it reopened in July 1927. The hut struggled to survive due to the political antagonism between Austria and Italy, with both armies camped out on the icy wastes of the Schwarzensteinsattel.

During World War 2 the hut was used to train alpine troops until it was forced to close from 1943 to 1948. When it reopened temporarily, it was virtually a wreck and unfit for use, having been plundered for its doors, windows and anything else that could be carried away.

Prior to demolition, the old hut was wardened by Gunther Knapp who had been the *Huettenwirt* for the past 35 years. A teacher by profession, Gunther was often seen with construction materials trying against all the odds to stop the hut from falling apart. Gunther was a man of many talents, organising the first hut in the Alps to have an internet page and live webcam. Moreover, perhaps his main attribute was that he was a master *Schnappsetier* (maker of schnapps), and he had lots of bottles of home-made schnapps stashed throughout the hut. As *Gastestube* (dining room) entertainer, in the ways of the Alte Sud Tirol, he would bring everything to a stop at 18:00 to sing the Sud Tirol anthem followed by a conga dance through the hut. With the mood set, dinner would then be served. His presence will long be remembered.

This is a brilliant, fun hut for all the right reasons in the *Gemuetlichkeit* (homely) tradition.

Tuxerjochhaus (2316m)

Location	Situated on the level platform of Tuxerjoch at the head of the Tuxertal valley, with a particularly fine view of the Olperer and Gefrorene-Wand-Spitzen
Transport	To Hintertux 2+hr then by Postbus 4104 to Mayrhofen: 09:30/10:30/10:55/11:30/12:30
Connections	Geraer Hut 6–7hr, Friesenberghaus 6–7hr, Lizumer Hut 5hr
Owner	Austrian Tourist Club OeTK
Open	From late June to end of September
Facilities	9B/26M/10N Excellent restaurant and toilet facilities and token-operated showers
Address	Franz Hotter, Tuxerjochhaus 798, A 6294 Tux, Austria
Tel	Hut (0043) 5287 87216 or (0043) 664 244 1714
Email	info@tuxerjochhaus.at, hotterfranz@gmx.at

Tuxerjochhaus

This superbly sited hut was built in 1910 by the Hotter family, who have been fine custodians of the hut ever since.

The hut is very popular with day visitors from Hintertux who make the effort to walk from the top of the Sommerbergalm cable-car station. However, by late afternoon most day visitors will have left, leaving the hut to those on the Peter Habeler or Olperer Runde Tours. Make sure you make your reservation early to avoid 'sleeping with the furniture' or having to descend to Hintertux for accommodation.

The hut has excellent facilities, including a particularly fine dining room extension with 180-degree panoramic windows with views in all directions but mainly dominated by the high peaks of the Gefrorene-Wand-Spitzen and the Olperer.

While the hut is mainly associated with skiing, it is enjoying a summer renaissance due to the increasing popularity of the Peter Habeler and Olperer Runde Tours.

This is a good, friendly hut very much in the *Gemuetlichkeit* (homely) tradition.

Day walk from Mayrhofen

Bus 4104 from Mayrhofen to the bus terminus at Hintertux Gletscherbahn. Bus times from Mayrhofen: 08:45/09:40/10:40; from Hintertux: 15:30/16:30/17:55/18:55/19:55

From the bus terminus at Hintertux take the Gletscherbahn cable-car up to the Sommerbergalm cable-car station complex. From here the most direct route is to follow the path that follows the service road on and off to the hut. **About 1hr**

Alternatively, at Sommerbergalm follow the service road heading off SW for ½km until it meets Route 326 on the Peter Habeler Runde Tour. Here turn right and follow the footpath across the hillside until it joins the hut's service road. Follow the service road or adjacent footpath to the hut. **About 1hr 20min** From the hut a short excursion can be made to the nearby Pfannkoepfl (2388m).

Return by the same route or the service road and various tracks back to the bus terminus at Hintertux.

APPENDIX A
Useful contacts

www.mayrhofen.at
www.zillertal.at
myZillertal.app

Websites
Some of these are currently in German but they will inevitably at some stage be translated into English:
www.Zillertal.at
www.alpenverein.de
www.mayrhofen.at
www.tirol.com
www.naturpark-zillertal.at
www.bergwelten.com

Information services
Austrian National Tourist Office
4th Floor,
54 Hatton Garden
London EC1N 8HN
tel 0044 20 3409 6616
tel 0800 400 200 00
email info@austria.info
www.austria.info/uk
Holiday service tel 0800 400 200 00
Austrian Alpine Club (UK)

Oesterreichischer Alpenverein Britannia
Unit 43, Glenmore Business Park
Blackhill Road, Holton Heath
Poole, Dorset BH16 6NL
tel 0044 1929 556870
email aac.office@aacuk.org.uk
www.aacuk.org.ukwww.alpenverein.at/
britannia

Austrian Alpine Club Head Office in Austria
Oesterreichischer Alpenverein
Alpenvereinhaus
Olympia Strasse
A 6020 Innsbruck
tel 0043 512 595470
www.alpenverein.at
email office@alpenverein.at

Mayrhofen Tourist Information Centre
Europahaus Congress Centre
Durster Strasse 225
A 6290 Mayrhofen
Austria
www.europahaus.at
email congress@europahaus.at
tel 0043 5285 6750
www.Mayrhofen.at
www.naturpark-zillertal.at

Public transport

Airlines
www.klm.com
www.austrianairlines.com
www.britishairways.com
www.tui.co.uk
www.easyjet.com
www.ryanair.com
www.aerlingus.com
www.lufthansa.com
www.jet2.com

Railways

German Railways
(DB: Deutsche Bundesbahn)
www.bahn.de

Austrian Railways
(OBB: Oesterreichische Bundesbahnen)
www.oebb.at

Zillertal Railway
(Zillertalbahn)
www.zillertalbahn.at

Verkehrsverbund Tirol
www.vvt.at

Bus services

Four Seasons Travel
A 6020 Innsbruck
www.tirol-taxi.at
email office@airport-transfer.com
tel 0043 512 584157

Postbus
www.postbus.at

Verkehrsverbund Tirol
www.vvt.at

Taxi services

Taxi Thaler
0043 5285 63423 or 0043 664 2006596

Taxi Kroll
0043 5285 62967

Floitentaxi
0043 664 102 93 54

Wipptal Taxi
0043 664 122 30 55

Accommodation in the valley

Gasthof Hotel Post in Jenbach and **Hotel Post** in Kaltenbach are recommended.

Should you wish to stay in Mayrhofen, **Der Siegeler** (tel 0043 664 341 0423, info@hotel-siegelerhof.at, www.hotel-siegelerhof.at), opposite the Europahaus Congress Centre and the main tourist information office, is within a five-minute walk from the railway station and provides good accommodation at a reasonable cost. The Gasthof is managed by Mike Thaler, who provides good, clean, inexpensive bed and breakfast accommodation.

The following hotels are highly recommended:

- **Hotel Pramstraller** – Located a five-minute walk from the Europahaus Congress Centre and tourist information centre on Durster Strasse, this first-class hotel is managed by the Pramstraller family (tel 0043 5285 62119, info@pramstraller.at, www.pramstraller.at)

- **Hotel Theresia** – Located in the nearby village of Bichl, five minutes by train or a 20-minute walk away, this excellent hotel is a find for those who treasure peace and quiet. The hotel is managed by Doris Gruber, who just loves to chit-chat with her British visitors (tel 0043 5282 3702, info@theresia.at, www.theresia.at)

Should you have to stay in Innsbruck, hotels can be booked from the tourist information centre located at the entrance to the main tourist area of the *Alte Stadt* (old town). In terms of places to stay, the following are recommended:

- **Hotel Mondschein** – Located just across the Inn Brucke bridge on the north side of the River Inn, less than five minutes' walk to the old part of the city the Alte Stadt (tel 0043 512 22784 or email office@mondschein.at, www.mondschein.at)
- **Nepomuks Backpackers Hostel** – Located just off the main square, in the old part of the Alte Stadt above the Konditorei cake shop. Highly recommended (tel 0043 664 7879197 or 0043 512 584118 or email mail@nepomuks.at, www. nepomuks.at)

If you have to stay overnight in Salzburg, then the family-run **Zur Post Hotel** (tel 0043 662 832339 or email hotelzurpost@EUnet.at) is recommended, located five minutes from the airport and a 15-minute walk from the centre of this fine old city.

If you find yourself having to stay overnight in Steinach at the start of the Zillertal South Tirol Tour, the **Zur Rose Hotel** (tel 0043 5272 6221, info@hotelrose.at, www. hotelrose.at) is recommended, located on the main street, just a 10-minute walk from the railway station. The hotel is managed by the Holzmann family, with master chef Franz providing an excellent choice of menu.

Medical

Doctors

In Mayrhofen there are three GPs on the *Hauptstrasse* (main street):

- Dr Gredler, tel 05285 62550
- Dr Schneidinger, tel 05285 63124
- Dr Zumtobel, tel 05285 62054

Dentists

Not the nicest things to think about, but if you need a dentist, these three practioners are available:

- Dr Manfred and Maximillian Reitmeir, tel 05285 63886
- Dr Olga Shafe Schimanek, tel 05285 63189
- Dr Pavel Kriz, tel 05285 63341

Hut information

For a partial searchable directory of mountain huts, with links to emails and websites where available, visit the following sites:

www.bergsteigen.com click 'Hutten'

www.alpenverein.at click 'Huts & Trails'

Professional mountain guides

Should you require the services of a professional mountain guide (*Bergfuehrer*), the following experts can be hired:

In Mayrhofen via Peter Habeler's Office
www.bergfuehrer-zillertal.at

My good friends:
Hannes Wettstein
cmeighoernewr@t-online.de

Robert Thaler
mail@alpinprofi.at

Peter Weber
bergerlebnis@edumail.at

Stefan Wierer
info@bergfuehrer-zillertal.at

British Association of International Mountain Leaders
www.baiml.org

APPENDIX B
German–English glossary

German	English
Mountain terminology	
Alm	alpine hut/pastures
Alpenvereins	Alpine Association (Club)
Bach/Wasserfal	river/stream/waterfall
Band/Grat/Kamm	ledge/ridge
Berg	mountain
Bergfuehrer	mountain guide
Bergrettung	mountain rescue
Eis	ice
Gefahrlich	dangerous
Gesprutt	route is closed/barred
Gipfel/Spitze	summit
Gletscher/Kees	glacier
Hinter/Mittler/Vorder	further/middle/nearer
Inner/Ausser	inner/outer
Kabel/Pickle	rope/ice axe
Kar	boulder field
Kessel/Grube	couloir/basin/combe
Links/Rechts/Geradeaus	left/right/straight ahead
Nadel	needle/pinnacle

German	English
Nord/Sud/Ost/West	north/south/east/west
Nur fur geubte	only for the experienced
Randkluft/Spalten	bergschrund/crevasses
Scharte/Sattel/Torl	col/saddle/pass/gate
Schweirig/Leicht	difficult/easy
See/Lac	tarn/lake
Steinslag	stonefall
Tal/Grund	valley
Uber/Unter	over/under
Wald/Baum	forest/tree
Wanderkarte	map
Weg	way/footpath
Wilde/Aperer	snow peak/rock peak
The weather	
Wetter	weather
Gewitter/Blitz	thunder storm/lightning
Kaiser Wetter/schlect wetter	good/poor weather
Regen/Sturmisch	rain/stormy
Sonnig	sunny
Wolkig/Nebel	cloudy/fog

German	English
When travelling	
Ankunft/Abflug/ Abfahrt	arrivals/ departures
Ausgang/Eingang	exit/entrance
Auskunft	information office
Bushaltestelle	bus stop
Einfach	one way/single
Fahrkarten Schalter	ticket office
Flughafen	airport
Gleis/Bahnsteig	platform
Hauptbahnhof	main railway station
Platz – Reservierung	booking office
Ruckfahrkarte/Hin und Zuruck	round trip/return
Ich moechte …	I would like …
Wo ist …?	Where is …?
Ich suche …	I'm looking for …
Selected menu list	
Mittag und Abendessen	lunch and dinner
Apfelstrudel	apple pie
Bergsteigeressen	potluck, low-cost climbers' meals served with a selection of vegetables or salad
Brot/Brotchen	bread/bread rolls
Compote	fresh or tinned fruit

German	English
Gemischter Salat	mixed salad
Gemuse	vegetables
Gruner Salat	green salad
Gulash	cubes of beef in a rich sauce
Jager Schnitzel	veal/pork fillets with mushroom topping
Kaiserschmarren	sweet pancakes
Kartoffel mit Spiegeleier	pan-fried potatoes with fried egg
Kartoffel-gaertreide- bratlinge mit Salat garniture	pan-fried potatoes with salad garnish
Kartoffel	potato
Kaese Brot	cheese bread
Kaesespaetzle	cheese with noodles
Knodelsuppe	soup with dumplings
Pfeffer	pepper
Reis	rice
Salz	salt
Schinken Brot	ham and bread
Senf	mustard
Spiegeleier und Schinken	fried eggs and ham
Tagesuppe	soup of the day
Tiroler Grotzl	fried potato and eggs
Vegetarische	vegetarian meals

German	English
Wiener Schnitzel	breaded veal/pork fillets
Wurst Brot	sausage and bread
Wurstsuppe	soup with sausages
Zweibelrostbraten	broiled or fried beef with onions

Other useful food-related words

German	English
Speisekarte	menu
Tasse	cup
Teller	plate
Schussel	bowl
Messer	knife
Gabel	fork
Loeffel	spoon
Bier	beer
Weiss/Rot Wein	white/red wine

German	English
Schnapps	clear, strong alcoholic spirit, aka rocket fuel
Tee/Kaffee/Milch	tea/coffee/milk
Limonade	lemonade
heiss/kalt	hot/cold
gross/klein	large/small
Viertel/Halbe	quarter/half

When ordering or paying

German	English
Wie bitte	Excuse me
Sprechen Sie Englisch?	Do you speak English?
Wie viel? Mein Rechnung bitte	How much? My bill please
Die Rechnung bitte	The bill please
Kann ich haben ...?	Can I have ...?
Haben sie ...?	Have you ...?
Haben sie vegetarische Gerichte Essen?	Do you have vegetarian meals?

APPENDIX C
Further reading

Hut directory
OeAV, AVS and DAV Bergverlag, *Alpenvereinshuetten Directory* (previously the Green book): *Volume 1 Ostalpen – Deutschland, Osterreich, Sudtyrol*, Rother (www.rother.de)

Maps
The following maps are required for the Zillertal Rucksack Route. The maps are published by the Austrian Alpine Club and available from the UK Section of the Austrian Alpine Club (UK).

Alpenvereinskarte Zillertal Alpen
- Sheet 35/1 Westliches (West), Scale 1:25,000
- Sheet 35/2 Mittler (Central), Scale 1: 25,000
  Also recommended, these two maps cover the complete region at a glance and are available from major map retailers:
- Freytag & Berndt Wanderkarte: Sheet 152 Mayrhofen, Zillertal Alpen, Gerlos-Krimml, Scale 1:50,000
- Kompass Wanderkarte: Sheet 37 Zillertaler Alpen: Tuxer Alpen, Scale 1:50,000

Books
OeAV Hut Directory (previously the Green book): *Volume 1 Ostalpen*, Rother (www.rother.de)
Dieter Seibert, *Eastern Alps: The Classic Routes on the Highest Peaks*, Diadem Books – includes the Hochfeiler, Grosser Loeffler, Grosser Moeseler, Olperer and Schwarzenstein
Zillertal Alpen: 50 Selected Walks (In German), Rother Wander Fuehrer
Trekking in the Alps, Cicerone Press Ltd (www.cicerone.co.uk)

Websites
These websites are mostly in German but are gradually being translated into English.
www.zillertal.at
www.alpenverein.de
www.naturpark-zillertal.at
www.mayrhofen.at
www.tirol.com
www.bergwelten.com

www.alpenvereinaktiv.com
www.outdooractive.com

Inspirational reading

You may find the following mountaineering books written by mountain lovers long ago interesting and inspiring – that is if you can track them down!

Smythe, Frank S, *Over Tyrolese Hills*, Hodder and Stoughton, 1936

Sir Martin Conway, *The Alps from End to End*, Nelson Books, 1894

Francis Fox Tuckett, *Pictures in Tyrol and Elsewhere*, Longmans, Green and Co., 1867

Felix Austria, Zillertal Alps by Philip Tallantire, Eden Press, 1971

NOTES

Berliner Hut	**Dominikus Hut Alpengasthof**	**Edelraut Hut**
Friesenberghaus	**Furtschaglhaus**	**Gams Hut**
Gasthof Stein	**Geraer Hut**	**Greizer Hut**

Hochfeiler Hut	Kasseler Hut	Karl von Edel Hut
Landshuter Europa Hut	Nevesjoch Hut	Olperer Hut
Pfitscherjochhaus	Schwarzenstein Hut	Tuxerjochhaus